MARCUS
J. BORG

THE

GOD

WE NEVER KNEW

BEYOND DOGMATIC
RELIGION TO A
MORE AUTHENTIC
CONTEMPORARY FAITH

HarperSanFrancisco
A Division of HarperCollinsPublishers

HarperSanFrancisco and the author, in association with The Basic Foundation, a not-for-profit organization whose primary mission is reforestation, will facilitate the planting of two trees for every one tree used in the manufacture of this book.

A TREE CLAUSE BOOK

HarperCollins books may be purchased for educational, business, or sales promotional use. For information please write: Special Markets Department, HarperCollins Publishers, Inc., 10 East 53rd Street, New York, NY 10022.

HarperCollins Web Site: http://www.harpercollins.com
HarperCollins,® 🔥,® HarperSanFrancisco™, and A TREE CLAUSE BOOK®
are trademarks of HarperCollins Publishers, Inc.

FIRST HarperCollins PAPERBACK EDITION PUBLISHED IN 1998
Book design by Ralph Fowler

Library of Congress Cataloging-in-Publication Data
Borg, Marcus J.
The God we never knew : beyond dogmatic religion to a more authentic contemporary faith /
Marcus J. Borg. — 1st ed.
Includes bibliographical references and index.
ISBN 0-06-061034-4 (cloth)
ISBN 0-06-061035-2 (pbk.)
1. Christianity—Miscellanea. 2. Christianity—Controversial literature. 3. Jesus Christ—Miscellanea. 4. Liberalism (Religion). 5. Borg, Marcus J. I. Title.
BR124.B67 1997
96-52871

03 02 01   RRD(H) 20 19 18 17 16 15 14

For Marianne
with whom I have learned
much about the sacred

CONTENTS

With this book on God, I venture beyond my area of academic specialization. As a Jesus scholar, I have focused my research and writing on the historical study of Jesus and Christian origins, and the implications of such study for Christian theology and life.

But though I am a Jesus scholar and not a God scholar, the subject of God has been with me for a very long time, indeed from long before I was even aware of historical Jesus scholarship. I grew up with God. Ever since, the subject and question of God—devotionally, intellectually, and experientially—has been central. I have been praising God, thinking about God, and yearning for God all of my life.

Thus, though I write about God as a nonspecialist, my interest is neither recent nor peripheral. As a professor of religious studies, I have taught courses about God for almost three decades. As a Jesus scholar, I have found it impossible to say very much about Jesus without also talking about God. Finally, my own Christian journey (from initial belief through doubt and unbelief to rediscovery and reformulation) has centered on the question of God.

This book thus comes out of my own journey, now more than five decades old, of living within the Christian tradition and seeking to make sense of it in a way that is faithful to both biblical and post-biblical traditions.

Because I am a nonspecialist, I do not see this book as a contribution to the scholarly discussion of God but as an accessible exposition of some quite general insights about the importance of how we think about God and image God—about how our concepts and images of God affect not only our notion of the sacred but our understanding of the religious life itself. How we think about God matters.

My perspective is cross-cultural and Christian. On the one hand, I make use of insights drawn from the cross-cultural study of religions—especially what they say about the sacred and experiences of the sacred. On the other hand, I focus especially on what Christianity (and the Bible) says about God. Most of my illustrations come from the Christian tradition, and the book centers on making sense of the Christian tradition by seeing it in a particular way as we move into the third millennium.

This dual perspective flows out of my vocational and existential commitments. The cross-cultural perspective comes from teaching religious studies in the pluralistic and quite secularized settings of a nondenominational private college and a public state university. In such settings, a cross-cultural approach is both natural and appropriate. Such an approach does not privilege any particular religious tradition, and does not depend on religious belief or commitment.

By Christian perspective, I refer to my own religious commitment and orientation. I am a Christian of a nonliteralistic and nonexclusivistic kind. As an Episcopalian, I am involved in the life of the church, living out my relationship to the sacred in a community that uses the language, symbols, and practices of the Christian tradition.

My Christian perspective accounts for this book's focus on the Christian tradition. It is what I know best. Moreover, most readers of this book are Christians, or on the margin of the church, or living in a culture shaped by Christianity. The book thus centers on the religious tradition with which most of us are best acquainted.

I see this book as an attempt to do Christian theology within the framework of religious pluralism and the cross-cultural study of religion. Given its Christian focus and audience, it is written primarily for Christians but also for anybody interested in listening in on a Christian conversation. The conversation is one that has been going on within myself, with other Christians in the present, and with Christian voices from the past. My own conviction, developed in this book, is that the Christian tradition, understood at a deeper level than what many of us learned, makes persuasive and compelling sense.

I want to acknowledge the particular occasions that contributed to the incubation of this book. Portions of it were delivered as the Collins Lectures at Trinity Episcopal Cathedral in Portland, Oregon, in March

1995, and I wish to thank Mary Beth Collins and the Collins Foundation for supporting these lectures. I wish also to thank the Pacific Center for Spiritual Formation and Francis Geddes for inviting me to treat the subject of God at Wellspring Renewal Center in Mendocino County, California, in the summer of 1995. In addition, I wish to thank Father Gordon McBride and Grace–St. Paul's Episcopal Church in Tucson, Arizona, for inviting me to do a lecture series on God in November of 1996.

I also wish to thank my graduate assistant, Mary Streufert, for her very able and helpful assistance with this project. She is soon to have her first baby and will then move on to a different institution for doctoral work. I will miss her.

MEETING GOD
AGAIN FOR
THE FIRST TIME

This book about "the God we never knew" describes an understanding of God—or "the sacred" or "Spirit," terms that I use synonymously and interchangeably—that is very ancient as well as particularly suited to our own time. It is grounded in experience, my own and the experience of others throughout the centuries, and integrated with the biblical and Christian tradition. Though quite unlike the understanding of God that I acquired growing up in the church, it is not "new" but is consistent with the theological tradition of Christianity.

I suppose the title of this book could be "The God *I* Never Knew," for it is to a considerable extent my own story. In it, I describe a way of thinking about God and living with God that I never knew as a child and young person, despite the fact that I grew up as a Christian.

I did not "see" this way of thinking about God and the religious life until I was in my thirties. I do not know the full explanation of why it took me so long. I may be slow-witted. But a major reason is that the notion of God I received as a child stood in the way. Because of my Christian upbringing, I thought I knew what the word *God* meant: a supernatural being "out there" who created the world a long time ago and had occasionally intervened in the aeons since, especially in the events recorded in the Bible. God was not "here" but "somewhere else." And someday, after death, we might be with God, provided that we had done or believed whatever was necessary to pass the final judgment.

My childhood notion of God, with refinements, persisted for about three decades. In childhood, I believed in this notion of God without difficulty; in my early teens, I began to have doubts about it; in my twenties, the doubts became disbelief; but through this whole process, the same notion of God persisted. It was what I believed and then disbelieved. Compared to that notion of God, the God I have come to know since is the God I never knew.

But I call this book "The God *We* Never Knew" because I do not think my experience was unique. Rather, many people in our time have experienced similar problems with the understanding of God they received as children growing up in a religious tradition.

As the twentieth century and the second Christian millennium draw to a close, an older way of understanding Christianity that nourished (and sometimes haunted) the lives of millions of people for over a thousand years has ceased to be persuasive to many in our time. More specifically, over the last thirty to forty years, an older way of thinking about God (and the Bible, Jesus, and Christianity itself) has ceased to be compelling to many Christians, especially those who are the natural constituency of mainline churches.

This older way was the "popular-level Christianity" of a previous generation.[1] In harder and softer forms, it was doctrinal, moralistic, literalistic, exclusivistic, and oriented toward an afterlife. In its view, being Christian meant believing that a certain set of doctrinal claims were true, and it meant seeking to live in accord with Christianity's ethical teaching. It tended to take the Bible and doctrine literally, unless there were compelling reasons not to. It typically affirmed that Christianity was the only way of salvation. And it defined salvation as "afterlife"—as going to heaven. Basically, then, Christianity was about believing in central Christian teachings *now* for the sake of heaven *later*.

This older way of understanding Christianity still worked for many of our parents and grandparents. But in the last half of the twentieth century, it has become less and less credible to many people, including many who are mainline Christians. Though fundamentalist and conservative Christians speak about this older understanding of God and the Bible with great confidence, what they have to say makes little sense to many of us. There are millions of people—within the church and the church alumni association, as well as some who have never been part of a church—for whom this older understanding of God and Christianity does not work.

For these, the chief obstacle to being a wholehearted Christian is thus intellectual: the tradition in the form in which they learned it doesn't make sense to them anymore. My own conviction, developed in this book, is the opposite: the Christian tradition, understood at a deeper level, makes persuasive and compelling sense. It is especially for people struggling with this issue that this book is written.

At the center of the book is God. I am persuaded that there is a lot of uncertainty and confusion about God in our culture and among our churches. Public opinion polls typically report that 95 percent of Americans say that they believe in God, an amazing percentage.[2] This might suggest considerable confidence in the reality of God, rather than uncertainty.

But the percentage conceals as much as it discloses. In his important study of the religious life of the "boomer" generation, Wade Roof notes that the high percentage glosses over "differences both in conceptions of God and in conviction" and that "recent studies indicate, for example, that levels of doubt and disbelief are often greater than the polls would suggest."[3] He then reports that among the boomer generation, 50 percent of high school graduates and 65 percent of those with postgraduate education sometimes doubt the existence of God.[4]

Uncertainty about God is particularly a problem among mainline Christians and churches. As everybody knows, mainline denominations have suffered a major decline in membership over the last thirty years. The causes are complex, but among the most important is doubt about the reality of God. Conservative churches have done relatively well in part because of their strong convictions about God, reflected not only in their preaching and teaching but also in their worship. In many mainline churches, on the other hand, there is a "Don't ask, don't tell" approach to the question of God, as C. Kirk Hadaway and David A. Roozen note in their recent study.[5] Importantly, they also report that some mainline congregations have been growing and that what they all have in common is this: they take God seriously. Congregations that are full of God are full of people.[6] The converse also seems to be true: churches that are uncertain about God will soon find their pews empty of people.

At the same time that many people are finding the Christianity of their childhood to be problematic, our culture is experiencing a surge of religious and spiritual interest. New Age movements, megachurches, the popularity of public television series on Joseph Campbell, Huston Smith, and Genesis, and the best-seller lists all disclose a large appetite for God and the spiritual life. Thus people remain interested in God, at the same time that many are finding unconvincing the beliefs that were once taken for granted by almost everybody in Western culture.

Hence this book about God. It is simultaneously autobiographical, theological, biblical, and experiential. Though it focuses on God, it also looks at much of what is central to the Christian life, including not only concepts and images of God but also Jesus, spirituality, social vision, and salvation. It has three parts: thinking about God, imaging God, and living with God.

It takes seriously several features of contemporary culture, including our culture's growing secularization of consciousness, which makes many people suspicious of religion as a set of doctrinal claims about the way things are. It also takes seriously our growing awareness of religious pluralism, which makes us suspicious of the claim that any one tradition is the only way. And it takes seriously the turn to experience that marks the spirituality of many in the modern world: what I come to know in my own experience can be trusted to be true in a way that what we learned secondhand from tradition cannot be trusted.

To provide an overview, Part One (Chapters One and Two) treats the issue of *how we think about God*. The premise of Part One (and to some extent of the book as a whole) is simple: how we think about God matters. It affects the credibility of religion in general and of Christianity in particular. Our concept of God can make God seem real or unreal, just as it can also make God seem remote or near.

How we think about God matters for a second reason as well. Because there is a close connection between images of God and images of the religious life, how we think about God affects how we see the religious life.

- Is the religious life focused on this life or the next (and if both, then in what proportion)?
- Is it about meeting God's requirements, whether they are many or few? Or about living by grace in a place beyond the dynamic of requirements?
- Does it lead to a preoccupation with our own salvation and goodness (or lack thereof)? Or to liberation from self-preoccupation?

- Does it result in an emphasis on righteousness and boundary drawing? Or is the emphasis on compassion and an inclusive social (and even ecological) vision?

- Is it about believing in a supernatural being "out there" or about being in relationship with a sacred reality "right here"?

I begin autobiographically, describing the understanding of God and Christianity I received as a child growing up in the church and then the "re-visioning" of the Christian tradition that has occurred in my adult life. In particular, I argue that a "panentheistic" concept of God offers the most adequate way of thinking about the sacred; in this concept, the sacred is "right here" as well as "the beyond" that encompasses everything. This way of thinking about God, I claim, is not only faithful to the biblical and Christian tradition but also makes the most sense of our experience. For there is much in our experience—of nature, human love, mystery, wonder, amazement—that conveys the reality of the sacred, a surpassingly great "more" that we know in exceptional moments. Many of us experience life as permeated and surrounded by a gracious mystery, a surplus of being that transcends understanding, and when we come to know that mystery as God, our faith becomes full of meaning and vitality. I include descriptions of varieties of religious experiences that point to the reality of the sacred.

Part Two (Chapters Three and Four) treats *how we image God*. Chapter Three explores a variety of biblical images of God and their effects on images of ourselves and of the religious life. In particular, I analyze the effects of the monarchical model or image of God (God as king, lawgiver, and judge) on Christian understandings of the religious life, nature, politics, and gender, and then look at the very different effects of alternative images of God in the biblical tradition. Chapter Four treats the role of Jesus in the Christian tradition as "the image of the invisible God." Here, I speak about both the historical Jesus and the canonical Jesus as disclosures of the sacred, as images of the invisible God.

Part Three (Chapters Five through Seven) concerns *living with God*. That is, if we accept the understandings of God and the religious life developed in Parts One and Two, what is life with God like? Chapter Five describes spirituality and a variety of spiritual practices as ways of "opening the heart" to God and nourishing the relationship with God.

Chapter Six, "The Dream of God," underlines the communal and political dimensions of the biblical tradition and argues that the Christian life as it matures will increasingly be captivated by and committed to an alternative social vision. Finally, in Chapter Seven, I describe a wide range of biblical images of salvation. Although I look at the question of an afterlife, I argue that the primary meanings of salvation have to do with our lives this side of death.

Thus, in addition to being centrally about God, this book is to some extent a Christian "primer"—an introduction to what seem to me to be the central elements of the Christian life as a life of relationship to the sacred.

To return to the cultural climate in which this book is written, I note that it is almost exactly two hundred years ago, in 1799, that a brilliant young German theologian named Friedrich Schleiermacher (1768–1834) wrote a book that is often cited as the fountainhead of modern Christian theology.[7] He addressed it to "the cultured despisers of religion." That is a harsh-sounding phrase, but Schleiermacher meant nothing insulting by it. He was referring to the educated elite of his time, a small minority whose thinking had been shaped by the emerging worldview of the Enlightenment, that revolution in Western intellectual history that generated the modern era. Scientific ways of knowing were beginning to replace sacred tradition and divine authority as the basis of knowledge.

In our time, most of us in the Western world have become "cultured despisers of religion," whether we know it or not. What belonged only to the educated elites two hundred years ago has become the widespread modern worldview—the taken-for-granted assumptions of our culture about what is real and what life is about.

Some of us resist the impact of the modern worldview by becoming fundamentalists, insisting on the truthfulness of premodern Christian ways of seeing things in spite of their conflicts with modern knowledge. Indeed, this very conflict prompted the birth of fundamentalism.[8]

Others of us seek to add the notion of God to the modern worldview. To an essentially Newtonian view of the universe as a gigantic machine, made up of tiny bits and pieces of "stuff" all operating in accord with natural laws, we add a notion of God as a supernatural being who created the whole but who is essentially outside the process, except for the rather extraordinary interventions recorded in the biblical tradition.[9] But this notion of God and God's relationship to the universe makes God distant. Most of the time, God is uninvolved and not here.

Others give up on the notion of God. For some, this happens consciously, because the notion of God begins to seem incredible and incapable of substantiation. For others, letting go of the notion of God is more functional than consciously thought out. God becomes largely irrelevant. The notion of God in fact plays no major role in their lives although they may agree in opinion polls that "God exists." They are practical atheists.

And still others seek to take seriously what the Christian tradition and other religious traditions say about God or the sacred, even as they also take seriously what we have come to know in the modern period, but without absolutizing it. They seek to integrate Christianity with modern and postmodern perceptions, producing a revisioning of Christianity. This is the path to which my own experience has led me, and this is what this book is about.

Almost a century ago, William James, in his classic *The Varieties of Religious Experience,*[10] distinguished between firsthand religious experience and secondhand religion. In this book, I seek to help readers make the transition from believing in (or rejecting) secondhand religion to experiencing firsthand a relationship with the sacred. It is both an invitation to a life with God and a guidebook to the central elements of the Christian vision of such a life.

Notes

1. By "popular-level Christianity," I mean simply the Christianity of most Christians (and nothing negative at all).

2. In comparison, Karen Armstrong, author of *A History of God* (New York: Knopf, 1994), reports that the figure for England is only 35 percent.

3. Wade Roof, *A Generation of Seekers: The Spiritual Journeys of the Baby Boom Generation* (San Francisco: HarperSanFrancisco, 1993), pp. 71–72.

4. Roof, *Generation of Seekers,* p. 73.

5. C. Kirk Hadaway and David A. Roozen, *Rerouting the Protestant Mainstream* (Nashville, TN: Abingdon Press, 1995), pp. 76–77.

6. Hadaway and Roozen, *Rerouting the Protestant Mainstream,* p. 86; see also pp. 82–89, 129–31.

7. Friedrich Schleiermacher, *On Religion: Speeches to Its Cultured Despisers,* ed. Richard Crouter (Cambridge, England: Cambridge University Press, 1988). Crouter provides a useful introduction to Schleiermacher as well as to this work. Though Schleiermacher's greatest influence has been in mainline Protestant theology, he has also affected Catholic theology.

8. Fundamentalism as a conscious and deliberate insistence on the literal and historical factuality of Scripture came into existence early in the twentieth century. Rather than being "traditional Christianity," it is a modern reaction to the worldview of the Enlightenment. I agree with its rejection of the modern worldview as an absolute, but I cannot agree with its attempt to establish the Bible as a source of divinely guaranteed factual knowledge.

9. Named after Sir Isaac Newton (1642–1727), the modern worldview and its effects will be discussed further in Chapter One.

10. William James, *The Varieties of Religious Experience,* ed. and intro. by Martin Marty (New York: Penguin, 1982); originally published in 1902.

PART 1

THINKING
ABOUT
GOD

CHAPTER 1

THINKING
ABOUT GOD:

THE GOD
I MET THE
FIRST TIME

How are we to think of God? Some intellectual questions may not matter much, but this one has major consequences. What is our concept of God (or the sacred, or Spirit, terms that I use interchangeably)? By "concept of God," I simply mean what we have in mind when we use the word *God*. All of us have some concept of God, whether vague or precise and whether we are believers or nonbelievers.

My central claim is very direct: our concept of God matters.[1] It can make God seem credible or incredible, plausible or highly improbable. It can also make God seem distant or near, absent or present. How we conceptualize God also affects our sense of what the Christian life is about. Is the Christian life centrally about believing, or is it about a relationship? Is it about believing in God as a supernatural being separate from the universe or about a relationship to the Spirit who is right here and all around us? Is it about believing in a God "out there" or about a relationship with a God who is right here?

In this chapter, I will introduce two different "root concepts" for thinking about God. Both are found in the Bible and the Christian tradition. They are fundamentally different. The first conceptualizes God as a supernatural being "out there," separate from the world, who created the world a long time ago and who may from time to time intervene within it. In an important sense, this God is not "here" and thus cannot be known or experienced but only believed in (which, within the logic of this concept, is what "faith" is about). I will call this way of thinking about God "supernatural theism." Widespread within Christianity, it is perhaps what a majority of people (both believers and nonbelievers) think of when they think of God. Some accept the existence of such a being, and some reject it. But it is the notion of God as a supernatural being "out there" that is being accepted or rejected.

The second root concept of God in the Christian tradition thinks of God quite differently. God is the encompassing Spirit; we (and everything that is) are in God. For this concept, God is not a supernatural being separate from the universe; rather, God (the sacred, Spirit) is a nonmaterial layer or level or dimension of reality all around us. God is more than the universe, yet the universe is in God. Thus, in a spatial sense, God is not "somewhere else" but "right here." I will call this concept of God "panentheism."[2] This way of thinking about God is found among many of the most important voices in the Christian theological tradition.

Both concepts of God have nourished Christian lives through the centuries. For most of that time, the majority of Christians thought of God within the framework of supernatural theism. There is nothing wrong with this. Thinking of God as a supernatural being "out there" is the natural inference from many biblical passages, as well as the natural language of worship and devotion. And for most Christians until recently, this posed no serious problem. But in our time, thinking of God as a supernatural being "out there" has become an obstacle for many. It can make the reality of God seem doubtful, and it can make God seem very far away. And many people are not aware that there is a second root concept of God within the Christian tradition—namely, panentheism.

So it was for me. Though I did not know about panentheism as another Christian option for thinking about God until I was in my thirties, it has since become of utmost importance. It resolved the central religious and intellectual problem of the first three decades of my life. Indeed, becoming aware of panentheism made it possible for me to be a Christian again. The story of my own Christian and spiritual journey thus involves the movement from supernatural theism through doubt and disbelief to panentheism. The God I have met as an adult is the God I never knew growing up in the church.

GROWING UP CHRISTIAN

My own story of how I met God the first time begins in a Lutheran church in a small town in northeastern North Dakota in the 1940s.[3] There I received a way of thinking about God that for a long time shaped what I thought being a Christian meant.[4]

God and church were important in my town of 1,400 people. Most of us were Lutherans or Catholics. A few belonged to Episcopal, Baptist, and Federated congregations. But I can't recall knowing anybody who wasn't a member of a church. In this sense, the small-town world of my childhood was still the world of Christendom: everybody was Christian.

My earliest memories of God are associated with Our Savior's Lutheran Church. It was a white wood-frame building, with the sanctuary on the main floor and Sunday school rooms in the basement, where church suppers were also held. We attended every Sunday, and my parents were among the lay pillars of the congregation. My siblings, already in high school when I was a preschooler, sang in the choir.

Many of my early memories of God are connected with the music of our worship services. Each Sunday, we sang "Holy, Holy, Holy" as the opening hymn. Its verses created a vivid sense of two realities, God in heaven and us on earth.

Its first verse spoke of us here on earth "early in the morning" gathered for worship of the thrice-holy three-personed God:

> Holy, holy, holy, Lord God almighty,
> Early in the morning our song shall rise to thee;
> Holy, holy, holy, merciful and mighty,
> God in three persons, blessed Trinity.

In the second verse, we were taken to heaven, where those who had died joined heavenly beings in adoration of God:

> Holy, holy, holy, all the saints adore Thee,
> Casting down their golden crowns around the glassy sea;
> Cherubim and seraphim falling down before Thee,
> Which wert, and art, and evermore shall be.

Its third verse spoke of why we on earth did not see God:

Holy, holy, holy, though the darkness hide Thee,
Though the eye of sinful man thy glory may not see;
Only thou art holy; there is none beside Thee,
Perfect in power, in love and purity.

The contrast between us and God's holiness, power, love, and purity was strong; seeing with "the eye of sinful man," we lived in a darkness of our own making.

Almost as frequently we sang the great seventeenth-century German Lutheran hymn of praise extolling God as lord and king:

Praise to the Lord, the Almighty, the King of creation!
O my soul, praise Him, for He is thy health and salvation!
All ye who hear,
Now to His temple draw near,
Join me in glad adoration.

The hymn that we sang as the collection plates were brought forward combined thanksgiving and gratitude:

Now thank we all our God,
With heart and hands and voices.
Who wondrous things hath done,
In whom His world rejoices.
Who from our mother's arms
Hath blessed us on our way
With countless gifts of love,
And still is ours today.

The most solemn moment for me each Sunday morning was provided by a short piece of music sung by the choir:

The Lord is in his holy temple;
Let all the earth keep silence before him.

I do not know why these words, and the somber mood in which they were sung, so affected me. I only know that they did.

Our celebrations of Christmas and Easter created a strong association in my mind between God and the wondrous. Christmas was filled with wonders: the special star, the wise men, the holy birth in the stable, the angels singing to the shepherds. I recall one Christmas Eve when as the sun was setting, I thought that maybe if I looked really hard, I would see the Star of Bethlehem.

The music of Christmas was magic:

Joy to the world, the Lord is come!
Let earth receive her king!

O little town of Bethlehem, how still we see thee lie . . .

From heaven above to earth I come!

Silent night, holy night; all is calm, all is bright . . .

Hark the herald angels sing, glory to the newborn king!

My favorite was a solo my sister sang: "O holy night, the stars are brightly shining; it is the night of our dear Savior's birth."

Easter also had its wonders: the empty tomb, the angels, Jesus appearing to his startled followers. "Christ the Lord is risen today," we sang with as much volume as our Scandinavian hearts could manage. And as we sang "Up from the grave he arose," our voices ascended the musical scale as the body of Jesus rose from the dead. God and the wondrous went hand in hand.

I don't remember being taught very much about God in Sunday school, though God was the presupposition of everything we learned. We memorized Bible verses because they were the Word of God. We learned the Ten Commandments because they were the law of God. We heard about the people of ancient Israel because of their covenant with God and about Jesus because he was the Son of God. Everything revolved around God.

GOD "OUT THERE"

Central to the story of how I met God the first time is my earliest visual image of God, which goes back to preschool days. When I thought of God, I thought of Pastor Thorson, the pastor of our church. He had gray hair (rather wavy, as I recall). He wore a simple black robe (our branch of Lutheranism rejected clergy ornamentation such as stoles and vestments). I remember him as a big man; I was thus startled about a year ago when I saw an old photo of him with our family. He was in fact a relatively small man, shorter than my mother and sisters.

But he was my earliest visualization of God. When I prayed, I visualized Pastor Thorson's face. I knew, of course, that he wasn't God; even as a preschooler, I would have said, "No," if someone had asked me if he were. But when I thought about God or prayed to God, I "saw" Pastor Thorson.

My visual image of God as Pastor Thorson provided the central ingredient for the "supernatural theism" of my childhood. It was an anthropomorphic (humanlike) image of God. I thought of God as a "person," just as Pastor Thorson was a person. To be sure, God was a remarkable kind of person. Unlike us, God was spirit and not flesh and was all-knowing, all-seeing, and all-powerful. Nevertheless, God was a "person," and to me that meant that God was a being separate from the world. Pastor Thorson, of course, was also male, although this didn't seem significant at the time. But it added to the picture: for me as a child, God was a malelike celestial being "out there"—the familiar "old man in the sky."

Much of what I heard in church was consistent with my visualization of God as Pastor Thorson. In words repeated every Sunday, I heard that God was "up in heaven." In the Lord's Prayer, we prayed, "Our father who art in heaven." In the Apostles' Creed, we declared our belief that Jesus ascended into heaven in order to sit at God's right hand. Heaven was where God was.

I also heard something about God that didn't fit this image. Namely, I heard (though not as often) that God was everywhere, or *omnipresent*. When I was very young, I didn't experience any tension between thinking of God as a supernatural being up in heaven and thinking of God as everywhere. But one day—I think I was in fourth grade—I remember wondering how this could be. How could God be everywhere present and also be up in heaven? I couldn't imagine how a person (even a supernatural person) could be everywhere. I resolved this theological conundrum by deciding that God was really up in heaven and thus not really everywhere.

But now I was puzzled about what God's omnipresence might mean. Over time, I began to understand it in two ways. First, I thought that maybe omnipresence meant that God "from heaven" could see everywhere. I thus saw God's omnipresence as a form of God's omniscience: God knew what was happening everywhere. God became the big eye in the sky. God knew everything we did. In this respect, God was like one of the quite secularized saints about whom we sang:

He sees you when you're sleeping,
He knows when you're awake;

He knows when you've been bad or good,
So be good for goodness' sake.

Second, I thought that perhaps omnipresence might mean that God could *decide* to be anywhere. I thus reduced God's omnipresence to God's ability to be anywhere God chose to be, including right here. But most of the time, God was not here; God was "out there." Supernatural theism—the notion of God as a supernatural personal being separate from the world—had won out.

GOD THE FINGER-SHAKER

Pastor Thorson shaped my childhood image of God in yet another way. He was a finger-shaker. I am not speaking metaphorically but literally: he actually shook his finger at us as he preached. Sometimes he even shook his finger while pronouncing the forgiveness of sins:

> Almighty God, our heavenly Father, hath had mercy upon us, and hath given His only Son to die for us, and for His sake forgiveth us all our sins.[5]

Those words, accompanied by a chastising finger, carried a message: though told we were forgiven, we knew it was a close call.

The memory of my childhood image of God as a finger-shaker intrigued me. I wondered how many other people received an image of God as a finger-shaker, metaphorically if not literally. I also realized how exactly this image of God fit the understanding of Christianity that had emerged in my childhood: God had requirements, and Christianity was about how to meet those requirements. The finger-shaking God was God the lawgiver and judge. Pastor Thorson's unadorned black robe drove the point home: Who else in our experience wears a plain black robe? Moreover, God as the big eye in the sky and God the finger-shaker went together very well: as all-knowing, God the lawgiver and judge knew everything we thought or did. But we could be saved by being Christian—that was the requirement.

MY END-OF-CHILDHOOD PACKAGE

By the end of childhood, my image of God—as a supernatural being who was a finger-shaker—was part of a larger "package understanding" of Christianity. My image of God and my image of Christianity went together. The larger package was a version of the popular Christianity of a previous generation mentioned in the introduction to this book. In my own package, formed in my mind by the age of twelve or so, seven elements were central: God, the Bible, us, Jesus, the way of salvation, faith, the afterlife.

1. *God.* God was foundational, of course. My model of God was supernaturalist and interventionist. God was "out there," had created the universe a long time ago, and now watched over it. Occasionally, God intervened in the world, especially in the events reported in the Bible.

2. *The Bible.* The Bible was a divine product. As the inspired Word of God, it came from God as no other book did. It told us what God wanted us to believe and how to live. It was the ultimate authority for both faith and morals.

3. *Us.* Though created in the image of God and loved by God, we were sinners because of our disobedience. Sinful and guilty, we deserved punishment. But God had provided a solution, and this was where Jesus fit in.

4. *Jesus.* As God's only son, Jesus was the means of our salvation. Born of a virgin and being both human and divine, he was also sinless. He died for us, and his death was the sacrifice that made forgiveness of our sins possible.

5. *The way of salvation.* Faith in Jesus was the only way of salvation, which made Christianity the only way. This left a lot of people out, but that's why we had missionaries: to reach the millions of souls who were perishing, lost in the shades of night.

6. *Faith.* Faith meant strong and correct belief. It meant believing what God wanted us to believe, as disclosed in the Bible. Faith as *strong* belief meant that doubt was the opposite of faith. Faith as *correct* belief meant believing the right things. For me, that meant believing as we Lutherans believed. This also left a lot of people out.[6]

7. *The afterlife.* Heaven and hell were central. Salvation meant going to heaven, but some people would go to hell. So fundamental was this notion that if somebody had been able to convince me at age ten or twelve that there was no afterlife, I wouldn't have had any idea why one should be a Christian. It was all about going to heaven.

In a sentence, the image of Christianity I internalized as a child was "Believe now, for the sake of heaven later." I took it for granted that this was the meaning of biblical passages such as "Believe in the Lord Jesus Christ and you will be saved,"[7] or the last line of John 3.16, perhaps the best known verse in the New Testament: "Whosoever believes in Jesus will have eternal life." The concluding words of the absolution of sins pronounced by Pastor Thorson each Sunday morning underlined the point: "He that believes and is baptized shall be saved." Christianity was about believing in God and Jesus in order to go to heaven.

I recognize that my childhood package has distinctively Lutheran elements in it, especially the emphasis given to faith and to faith as correct belief. Yet I have found that many Christians from other denominations also recognize the package. With slight variations, it is the understanding of Christianity that many of us—whether Protestant, Catholic, or Orthodox—internalized as children.

Its two central elements are the same two that dominated my religious thinking during childhood: the God of supernatural theism (God "out there") and the God of requirements (God the "finger-shaker"). I thought of God as "somewhere else" (not here), salvation as "sometime else" (not now), and that there was something one had to do in order to be saved (that is, to go to heaven). Minimally, one had to be a Christian—that seemed clear. But was that really enough? Was it enough simply to be a Christian through baptism? And so it seemed important to be a "good Christian," whatever that might mean.

This combination—the God of supernatural theism and the God of requirements—thus generated an image of Christianity as a religion of meeting requirements now for the sake of eternal rewards later. There were different opinions about what those requirements were and whether they were many or few. But requirements there were, and a reward there would be. We were to be judged, whether by a weighing of our deeds, the integrity of our repentance, an assessment of our faith, or some combination; and on that judgment, our eternal destiny would depend.

Because this image of God and the Christian life was presented to me as divine revelation of the way things are, it went much deeper into my psyche than much of what I learned as a child. But this package understanding of Christianity began to come apart as I grew beyond childhood, as it did for many who grew up in the church.

GROWING UP IN THE ENLIGHTENMENT

For me, it came apart because of a collision between two worldviews. A worldview is a culture or religion's taken-for-granted understanding of reality—a root image of what is real and thus of how to live. A world-view is "the story of the universe that a culture accepts."[8] The package understanding of Christianity that my socialization taught me was the Christian worldview of "the Age of Faith," which M. Scott Peck has recently described in the noninclusive language of that age:

> Most central was faith in a single God who not only created the Universe but ultimately did so for the sake of the sustenance of human beings whom He loved so much that in the form of His only begotten son, Jesus Christ, He came down to live and die as one of us, thereby laying upon us an obligation to live our lives in constant worship of Him and adoration of Jesus.[9]

But I was also growing up in "the Age of Reason" and internalizing another worldview. What is called "the modern worldview" is the image of reality that emerged during the Enlightenment, the great divide in the intellectual history of the West that began in the seventeenth century and that separates the modern period from everything that went before it. Prior to the Enlightenment, the vast majority of humankind took it for granted that there were minimally two kinds or layers of reality: a spiritual kind and a material kind. A recent exhibition recounting the history of King's College chapel in Cambridge, England, put it compactly: "The people who built this chapel (in the late Middle Ages) thought of the universe, the whole of what there is, as twofold."

The Enlightenment, with its emphasis on scientific ways of knowing, gave birth to the modern worldview with its image of reality as essentially "onefold"—that is, as material. What is real is the world of matter and energy within the framework of the space-time continuum, self-contained and operating in accord with "natural laws" of cause and effect.[10] Essentially a Newtonian view of the universe, it has been superseded in the world of physics, but it was (and is) the worldview of popular modern culture.

In the mid-twentieth-century world in which I grew up, the modern worldview was everywhere. It was part of the air that I breathed, even though it was never explicitly taught or named. I cannot recall a teacher ever saying, "Today we're going to learn about the modern worldview."

Rather, it was the cumulative product (and foundation) of all that we learned. In elementary school, I remember being taught that everything was made up of molecules and atoms. A molecule was the smallest unit of a compound, and a molecule was made up of atoms (which were the smallest units of an element). Atoms in turn were made up of smaller parts yet: electrons, protons, and neutrons. What emerged was a picture of reality as made up of tiny bits and pieces of stuff—an essentially material understanding of reality.

I also learned about natural laws—that these bits and pieces of stuff interacted with each other in ways that were uniform and that could be described. This gave me a picture of reality as a gigantic and intricate machine, made up of smaller and smaller parts, all functioning together.

At the same time that my view of reality was becoming more material, my vision of the universe expanded enormously in both time and space. I learned that the earth was very old—I think dinosaurs were the trigger. I also learned that the universe was huge, maybe even infinite. I was fascinated by astronomy. My new awareness of the great size of the universe and the vast number of galaxies initially increased my sense of awe about God, though that was not to last.

The internalization of the modern worldview began to create doubts about my childhood faith, especially the two main ingredients of its picture of God: the God of supernatural theism and the God of requirements. I struggled with both.

In my early teens, I began to have serious doubts about the existence of God as a being "out there." I have written elsewhere about the fear, guilt, anguish, and prayers that my doubts generated.[11] Here I wish to emphasize the effect they had on my understanding of faith. When I was a child, faith (understood as believing in God, Jesus, and the Bible) took no effort. The central authority figures in my life told me that God was real and that Christianity was true, and I had no reason to think otherwise. When I was in my teens, faith began to mean believing claims that went beyond what we knew and—as my doubt increased—that seemed highly unlikely to be true. But, I thought, that's why we talk so much about faith: faith meant believing the improbable. That was the requirement: to believe in God in spite of all the reasons not to. Yet I was finding this increasingly difficult to do.

My situation was complicated by the onset of sexual awareness. I confused adolescent sexual curiosity with lust, which I had learned was really bad. It was the same as adultery: "Whoever lusts after a woman in his heart has committed adultery with her already."[12] I saw my sexual fantasies as "impure thoughts" and thus sinful (I was, of course, confusing my Lutheran superego with God). But I could not stop my impure thoughts, any more than I could stop my doubts. Both seemed like sins on my part, and my repeated contrition and repentance did not seem genuine; after all, I knew better, yet I still didn't change. My inability to control either seemed to confirm that I didn't take God seriously.

By my college years, the conflict between the material worldview of the Enlightenment and the supernatural theism of my Christian worldview was acute. It left me in a state of considerable perplexity and growing atheism (though I was largely unaware of the latter). The two pictures of reality didn't seem to fit together.

Within a material understanding of reality, what does one make of a being who is nonmaterial and "out there"? God began to seem unreal.

If the universe was governed by natural laws, what became of "the wondrous" that had been such a major element in my childhood faith? I could imagine the stories of God's wondrous activity in the Bible only as divine interventions by a being who was outside the natural process. The wondrous became the naturally impossible, and the impossible became the province of God. Moreover, in my experience such events didn't happen anymore. The wondrous thus became a thing of the past; it was the way God had acted in ancient times. The activity of God was then, not now.

And if the universe was enormous, maybe even infinite, where did a God "out there" fit in? Either I had to think of God as a being within the universe (which made no sense to me) or else as "beyond" the universe (which made God very far away, at best). The bigger the universe got, the farther away God seemed. God began to seem quite remote.

By the time I was in college, I had become a "deist" without knowing it. "Deism" was a theological position that emerged in the seventeenth and eighteenth centuries as an accommodation between the Enlightenment worldview and supernatural theism. (It was actually the view of many of our founding fathers, including Washington and Jefferson, despite what the ideologues of the Christian right want us to believe.) I discovered that I was a deist during a Sunday evening religious discussion group when I was a freshman. I offered the opinion that one could reconcile belief in God with modern science by saying that God created the universe in the beginning and that it had run in accord with natural laws ever since. A philosophy professor commented that this was the view held by the deists. I was surprised to learn that there was a name for the position I had articulated, and a little deflated about being so easily pigeonholed.

Without knowing it, I was reliving the history of modern thought in my own experience. In my childhood, I lived within a premodern worldview; in high school and college I lived through the Enlightenment. I also find it interesting that deism (both historically and in my own experience) was a halfway house on the way to atheism. There is little difference between a distant and absent God and no God at all.

Vague notions of an afterlife persisted. Judgment seemed less threatening, not because I had understood the notion of grace but because I was pretty doubtful about God.

Nevertheless, I went to seminary, motivated by intellectual fascination. In retrospect, I can see that the hound of heaven was after me and "knew" that the way to reach me at that stage of my life was through my head. But initially, seminary only deepened my doubt. There I learned two things about God that exacerbated the problem. On the one hand, much of what I heard reinforced my notion that the word *God* referred to a supernatural being "out there." Protestant theology in the early 1960s was still dominated by a movement known as neo-orthodoxy whose principal spokesperson was Karl Barth, one of the two most important Protestant theologians for much of this century. Barth was known for his emphasis on God's radical "transcendence," the technical term for God's "otherness."

One of Barth's most famous phrases was "God is *wholly other.*" If one knew nothing else about Barth, one knew at least that phrase. In retrospect, I'm not sure how Barth meant it, but I know how I heard it: to me it meant that God was a being separate from the universe and beyond the universe. My image of God was still importantly shaped by my childhood. Though I no longer visualized God with Pastor Thorson's face, I still thought that the word *God* referred to a personlike being "out there."

On the other hand, I also learned that the problems I had with supernatural theism were not unique to me. Indeed, there were theologians who sharply challenged this notion as an obstacle to being Christian. I recall the excitement with which I read the controversial best-seller *Honest to God* by John Robinson, a bishop of the Church of England.[13] Robinson argued that the notion of a God "up there" or "out there" had become incredible in the modern world. He spoke of "the end of theism" (by which he meant the end of "supernatural theism"). He also argued for an alternative way of thinking about God, which he as a Christian and bishop affirmed: rather than God being "out there" in the heights, God is known in the depths of personal experience.

I also read Paul Tillich (commonly regarded as the other most important Protestant theologian of the time, alongside Barth). Tillich attacked the God of supernatural theism by arguing that God was not *a* being but "*Being-Itself*" or "*the ground of being.*" He denied that God existed (and affirmed instead that "God is") by pointing out that "to exist" means to stand out from the ground of existence as a separate being. "Things" (stones, stars, people, and so on) exist by being separate things. God does not exist in that sense; rather, God *is*. Tillich attacked "the God of theological theism" (supernatural theism) as "bad theology." According to Tillich, this point of view is wrong because it sees God as "a being beside others and as such a part of the whole of reality." But God is not a part of reality but is "ultimate reality." Indeed, Tillich even argued that the natural and justifiable consequence of thinking of God as a separate being is atheism. Thus, for Tillich, God is "the God above God"—the God who remains when the God of supernatural theism disappears.[14]

I found Robinson and Tillich very appealing. Their attacks on supernatural theism legitimated the difficulties I was having. Tillich's claim that supernatural theism led to atheism fit my own experience.

But I was still unable to understand their affirmations very well. Robinson's claim that God was known in the depths of personal experience seemed to me to make God a metaphor for the deeply personal. Tillich's characterizations of God as "the ground of being" or "Being-Itself" or "ultimate reality" seemed to make God very impersonal. There were jokes about praying to "the ground of being."

My inability to understand their affirmations stemmed to some extent from the fact that the modern worldview continued to dominate my thinking. I knew no reality but the material. The notion of God therefore could not refer to anything more.[15] The modern worldview had become in my mind not simply an image of reality but a lens through which I saw reality. I had become a "fact fundamentalist," an Enlightenment fundamentalist.[16]

Though the question of God was the crucial one, I also had difficulties with other parts of my childhood understanding of Christianity. Regarding the Bible, the process was gradual. Though my family and church were not biblical fundamentalists, we were "natural literalists": we took it for granted that what the Bible said was factually true.[17] In elementary school, I wondered how to reconcile the Bible's six-day creation story with what I was learning about the age of the earth from fossils. I recall thinking, "Well, maybe each day was a very long period of time—a geological epoch." Thus I was able initially to affirm both the Bible and what I was learning in my science classes. I employed the same strategy as scientific creationists do; I assumed that the Bible as a divine product was of course factually true and would be seen by us to be so if only we interpreted it correctly.

The next step in my understanding of the Bible took place in seminary. There I let go of the notion that the Bible is a divine product. I learned that it is a human cultural product, the product of two ancient communities, biblical Israel and early Christianity. As such, it contained their understandings and affirmations, not statements coming directly or somewhat directly from God. The creation stories in the book of Genesis were Israel's stories of creation, not God's stories of creation. I realized that whatever "divine revelation" and the "inspiration of the Bible" meant (if they meant anything), they did not mean that the Bible was a divine product with divine authority.

Seminary also introduced me to the historical study of Jesus and Christian origins. I learned from my professors and the readings they assigned that Jesus almost certainly was not born of a virgin, did not think of himself as the Son of God, and did not see his purpose as dying for the sins of the world. But I have written about all this elsewhere.[18]

I also found the claim that Jesus and Christianity were the only way of salvation to be troublesome. When I was a child living in a town where everybody was Christian, this was not difficult. Everybody had a chance. But the more I became aware of the hundreds of millions of people in the past and the present who had lived beyond the reach of the Christian message, the more difficult it was to believe that they were all going to hell. It seemed radically unfair. Now, I would add, it seems incredible to think that the creator of the whole universe would choose to be known in only one religious tradition (which, fortunately, just happens to be our own). Such a claim also seems impossible to reconcile with the grace of God.

But the central problem remained God. Despite having read Robinson and Tillich, I continued throughout my twenties to think that the word *God* referred to a supernatural being "out there." I could imagine no other meaningful content for the notion. Perhaps this was because I was slow-witted, but it was also certainly because of the dominance of supernatural theism in Christianity as I knew it. The concept of God with which I struggled into my thirties has been the way popular Christianity over the centuries has most commonly thought of God. It is so widespread that it is often referred to as "the god of conventional Western theism" or "the generic idea of God" or "classical theism" or "traditional theism,"[19] even though it is not in fact the classical position of orthodox Christianity.

GOD AS TRANSCENDENT AND IMMANENT

The Christian tradition, on the other hand, has throughout its history consistently affirmed that God is both *transcendent* and *immanent,* two semitechnical theological terms that are helpful for thinking this through. The transcendence of God refers to God's "going beyond" the universe, God's otherness, God as more than the universe. God's immanence, on the hand, means God's presence in everything or nearness to everything. Immanence means to dwell with or within, as its Latin root *manere* suggests (from which, for example, we also get "mansion"). The immanence of God thus means the omnipresence of God.

The two root concepts of God I have described in this chapter are the product of different ways of emphasizing transcendence and immanence. *Supernatural theism* emphasizes only God's transcendence and essentially denies the immanence of God. God is other than the world and separate from the world. God is "out there" and not here. *Panentheism* affirms *both* the transcendence and immanence of God. It does not deny or subordinate one in order to affirm the other. For panentheism, God is both more than the universe and yet everywhere present in the universe.

What I heard as a young child—God is both "up in heaven" and "everywhere," "out there" and "right here"—was thus implicitly panentheistic (though the term was never used). But just as later in childhood I began to think of God as essentially "out there," as wholly transcendent, so also popular Christianity has most often emphasized primarily God's transcendence. When transcendence alone is emphasized, the result is supernatural theism.

The reasons why this concept of God is so common are easy to understand. Much of the language of the Bible and of Christian devotion creates the impression that God is a supernatural being separate from the world. The story of creation in the first chapter of Genesis is commonly understood as an act that took place a long time ago, "in the beginning," whereby God created a universe separate from God.[20] The biblical accounts of extraordinary miracles are naturally heard as stories of divine intervention from "outside" the natural order. New Testament passages about God "sending" Jesus to this world imply that God is somewhere else. The language of Christian devotion, which speaks of God as an anthropomorphic being separate from us whom we may address in prayer and adore in praise, reinforces this way of thinking.[21]

It is also easy to see why this concept of God was not a problem throughout much of Christian history. Prior to the sixteenth century, most people thought of the universe as relatively small. The earth was at its center, the stars and planets were not very far away, and thus to think of God as "up there" or "out there" did not make God seem unreal or remote. In the world of pre-Enlightenment Christendom, this concept of God, far from being an obstacle, was the commonsense meaning of Christian language.

Ironically, although the birth of the modern worldview in the Enlightenment posed major problems for this concept of God, its immediate consequence was a greater theological emphasis on the transcendence of God (and thus on supernatural theism). A recent book argues persuasively that beginning in the seventeenth century, theologians and philosophers increasingly "domesticated" the transcendence of God. The meaning of transcendence changed from referring to the "moreness" and mystery of God and the inadequacy of all human categories as applied to God, to referring to God as spatially distant from the world. An understanding of transcendence developed that made transcendence and immanence mutually exclusive opposites. Within this framework, the more transcendent God was, the less immanent.[22]

The greater emphasis on divine transcendence was accompanied by "the disenchantment of nature" brought about by scientific ways of knowing.[23] The emerging picture of the universe as a closed system operating in accord with natural laws of cause and effect progressively edged God out of the world. God thus had no place to be except "beyond" the universe.

The two primary theological options of the seventeenth and eighteenth centuries illustrate this development. "Deism" (the position I had unknowingly reached by college) affirmed that God created the universe and its laws at the beginning of time, but since then has been uninvolved in it. Deism therefore denied that miracles could happen and sought rational explanations for the miracle stories in the Bible. The theological opponents of deism, sometimes called "orthodox" and sometimes "supernaturalists" (the overlapping of the two terms in this period of history makes the point that "supernaturalism" and "orthodoxy" became identified), argued that the biblical miracles were supernatural interventions by God. But both deists and supernaturalists alike thought of God as "out there" and not here.

Thus, at a time when supernatural theism was becoming more problematic, it was also becoming more entrenched in Christian thinking. A recent writer speaks of it as *the* Christian position: the concept of "a personal God who transcends the world (that is, who is external to it and superior to it)" is "that of Christianity" and "generally accepted by Christian philosophers." Detractors of Christianity agree: it is "the conception to which atheistic philosophers generally refer in order to reject it."[24]

Another writer notes that the notion of "a Supreme Being is so firmly established in Western minds that the use of the word 'God' almost automatically conveys the idea of 'somebody up there.' "[25] It is the concept of God most often in mind when the question is asked, "Does God exist?" Most people understand the question to mean "Is there, in addition to all of the entities that make up the universe, another entity, namely God?"

The consequences of supernatural theism for my religious life as a Christian were severe. Four were particularly important. It made believing in God difficult, as it has for many people. God became remote at best, unreal at worst. The question of whether I was a believer or an atheist became the question of whether I believed in the God of supernatural theism. It also made the problem of evil acute. If one thinks of God as an all-powerful being who can intervene in the world at will (as this way of thinking about God most commonly does), then it follows that God could have intervened to stop the Holocaust and a whole host of other collective and personal disasters but chose not to. It is difficult to believe in such a God. It also affected my sense of what the Christian life was about. Because I thought of God as remote, "up in heaven," and not here, I thought Christian faith was about believing in a distant God; indeed, this became the central meaning of faith. Finally, it made prayer problematic. I could see no framework within which prayer made sense. It seemed like addressing a distant God who might not be there—like speaking into a universe that might be empty.

Thinking about God within the framework of supernatural theism was thus the primary issue and obstacle in my spiritual and religious life from late childhood into my early thirties. I now see that the concept of God that I took for granted was in fact a serious misunderstanding that made it impossible for me to take seriously that God was real.

For me, the problem was thus centrally intellectual, even though it deeply affected the rest of my life. For a variety of good reasons, not everybody experiences a serious intellectual problem with the notion of God. But some do. For my own religious journey, the resolution of the intellectual problem was indispensable; without it, I would still be on the outside of the Christian life looking in.

By the time I was thirty, like Humpty Dumpty, my childhood faith had fallen into pieces. My life since has led to a quite different understanding of what the Christian tradition says about God, and thus to a quite different understanding of the Christian life itself. I have realized that one may be an atheist regarding the God of supernatural theism and yet be a believer in God conceptualized another way, namely in the way offered by panentheism. This is the God I never knew. And this way of thinking about God—and the image of the Christian life that goes with it—are what the rest of this book is about.

Notes

1. In her richly and deservedly praised prizewinning book *She Who Is: The Mystery of God in Feminist Theological Discourse* (New York: Crossroad, 1992), Elizabeth Johnson says that the question,

"What is the right way to speak of God?" is "a question of unsurpassed importance" (p. 3). Similarly, Kenneth Leech, *Experiencing God: Theology as Spirituality* (San Francisco: Harper & Row, 1985), says that an inadequate view of God is more serious than atheism (p. 8).

2. For further clarification of panentheism (and how it differs from pantheism, with which it is sometimes confused), see Chapter Two in this book. Some theologians use other terms for panentheism, though the underlying concept is the same. For example, John Macquarrie, in *In Search of Deity: An Essay in Dialectical Theism* (New York: Crossroad, 1985), calls it "dialectical theism"; David Griffin, in *God and Religion in the Postmodern World* ([Albany: State University of New York Press, 1989], pp. 3, 90), calls it "naturalistic theism" (which he distinguishes from both "supernaturalistic theism" and "nontheistic naturalism"). Several refer to it as "dipolar theism" (a theism that affirms that God is more than the universe, even as it also affirms that God is "right here"). Among recent writers who call it panentheism are Elizabeth Johnson, *She Who Is*, and Sallie McFague, *Models of God* (Philadelphia: Fortress, 1987) and *The Body of God* (Minneapolis: Fortress, 1993).

3. For other autobiographical accounts of thinking about God, see especially Roberta Bondi's fine book, *Memories of God* (Nashville: Abingdon, 1993), and Thomas V. Morris, ed., *God and the Philosophers: The Reconciliation of Faith and Reason* (New York: Oxford University Press, 1994).

4. To get in touch with the religious impressions we formed in childhood is interesting and illuminating. For adult groups, I find the following questions especially useful: What are your earliest childhood memories associated with God? With what are they associated (church, Sunday school, family, or . . . ?)? Do any prayers or hymns stand out in your memory? When you were a child did you visualize God and, if so, how? What impression did you get of what God wanted from us? By the end of childhood, what "package understanding" of God and Christianity had formed in your mind?

Of course, one can continue the process beyond childhood. What happened to your notion of God and religion during your teen years? During your twenties? Is there a period in your life when your thinking about God changed significantly? How do you think of God now? And how satisfactory do you find your current thinking? Do you have any perplexities or unresolved conundrums?

5. From *The Lutheran Hymnary,* published in 1912.

6. It excluded all non-Christians, of course. About non-Lutheran Christians, we weren't sure. Presbyterians, Congregationalists, and Methodists were marginal. I can't recall that we even talked about Episcopalians. Roman Catholics were clearly out. But what matters for my point is not the very nonecumenical prejudices of fifty years ago but that faith was "correct belief," which meant believing in our particular version of Christianity.

7. Acts 16.31; see also Acts 4.12 and Rom. 10.9.

8. Griffin, *God and Religion in the Postmodern World,* p. 14. Griffin is especially helpful on the importance of worldviews and the conflict between the modern worldview and traditional religious belief, as are W. T. Stace, *Religion and the Modern Mind* (Philadelphia: Lippincott, 1952), and Huston Smith, *Forgotten Truth* (San Francisco: HarperSanFrancisco, 1976 and 1992). See also Chapter Six in my *Jesus in Contemporary Scholarship* (Valley Forge, PA: Trinity Press International, 1994), "Root Images and the Way We See," pp. 127–39.

9. M. Scott Peck, *In Search of Stones* (New York: Hyperion, 1995), pp. 5–6.

10. This is sometimes called the "scientific worldview." But strictly speaking, this term is inaccurate. There is nothing about science as a way of knowing that leads intrinsically to a material understanding of reality. Rather, a material understanding of reality is the product of the inference that only that which can be known scientifically may be regarded as real. See Smith, *Forgotten Truth,* pp. 16–17, 96–97, for an illuminating discussion of this point; "scientism" is his term for what happens when this inference is made. There is thus no necessary conflict between science and the claims of religion, though there is between scientism and religion.

11. See my *Meeting Jesus Again for the First Time* (San Francisco: HarperSanFrancisco, 1994), pp. 7–8.

12. Matt. 5.28.

13. Robinson, *Honest to God* (London: SCM Press, 1963; Philadelphia: Westminster, 1963). In addition to being an Anglican bishop, Robinson was also a well-known New Testament scholar. *Honest to God* has sold over a million copies and has been translated into seventeen languages. For the

controversy it caused, see David Edwards, ed., *The* Honest to God *Debate* (Philadelphia: Westminster, 1963); and Eric James, *A Life of Bishop John A. T. Robinson* (Grand Rapids, MI: Eerdmans, 1987), pp. 110–50. See also Robinson's *Exploration into God* (Stanford, CA: Stanford University Press, 1967).

14. Paul Tillich, *The Courage to Be* (New Haven, CT: Yale University Press, 1952), pp. 182–90, esp. pp. 184–85.

15. In David Griffin's fine phrase, I was able to hear Robinson and Tillich only as providing "a religious gloss over secularism's nihilistic picture of reality" (Griffin, *God and Religion in the Postmodern World,* p. 1). I do not think this is what Tillich and Robinson were doing, but that's all I was then able to understand.

16. For the phrase "fact fundamentalist," see Huston Smith in Marcus Borg, ed., *Jesus at 2000* (Boulder, CO: Westview, 1997), pp. 116–17.

17. "Natural literalism" is quite different from "conscious literalism." "Natural literalism" was the way most of our ancestors a few generations ago understood the Bible. They read it literally "naturally," without difficulty, because no problems with a literal reading were experienced. "Conscious literalism," on the other hand, insists on a literal reading because of an awareness of other ways of looking at the Bible. Fundamentalism is thus "conscious literalism" and is a modern movement; it emerged in the early twentieth century as a way of countering nonliteral ways of seeing the Bible. For the distinction, see Paul Tillich, *Dynamics of Faith* (New York: Harper & Row, 1952), pp. 51–53, and my use of it in *Jesus in Contemporary Scholarship,* pp. 174–78.

18. See *Meeting Jesus Again for the First Time* and *Jesus: A New Vision* (San Francisco: HarperSanFrancisco, 1987).

19. See Kenneth Leech, *Experiencing God,* p. 7, for "the god of conventional Western theism." Leech also calls this concept "God as super-object," p. 6. For "the generic idea of God," see David Griffin, *God and Religion in the Postmodern World,* p. 52. Elizabeth Johnson, a Roman Catholic theologian, in her important book *She Who Is,* p. 19, calls it "classical theism" and defines it as "the understanding that there is God (contrary to atheism), that God is one (contrary to polytheism), and that the one God is not to be identified with the world (contrary to pantheism). . . . [It] views God as the Supreme Being who made all things and rules all things." Anglican theologian John Macquarrie, in *In Search of Deity,* uses both "traditional theism" and "classical theism" to refer to thinking of God "as separate from and external to the world" (p. 7), "as one-sidedly transcendent, separate from and over or above the world" (p. 31). See also Dorothee Soelle, *Thinking about God* (Philadelphia: Trinity Press International, 1990), esp. Chapter Fourteen. All of these books offer excellent critiques of supernatural theism and expositions of the alternative.

20. I say "commonly" because there is another possibility. Namely, it is possible within the framework of supernatural theism to imagine creation as a continuing activity of God, even as God is thought of as essentially separate from the created universe. But usually creation is thought of as happening "in the beginning."

21. To avoid a possible misunderstanding and because I am going to argue for a different model of God, I wish to add that there is nothing wrong with the use of anthropomorphic and personal language in Christian devotion. What is important is that this language not be literalized into a concept.

22. William C. Placher, *The Domestication of Transcendence: How Modern Thinking About God Went Wrong* (Louisville, KY: Westminster John Knox, 1996). See esp. pp. 6–7, 111–12, 128–45, and his concluding paragraph on p. 215. Placher credits the notion of "contrastive transcendence" to Kathryn Tanner, *God and Creation in Christian Theology: Tyranny or Empowerment?* (Oxford, England: Basil Blackwell, 1988). Kenneth Leech, *Experiencing God,* p. 6, calls this notion of God "God as super-object" and also attributes it to the Enlightenment.

23. See the use of this phrase from Max Weber by Harvey Cox, *The Secular City* (New York: Macmillan, 1965), pp. 21–24.

24. Dominique Morin, *How to Understand God,* trans. by John Bowden (New York: Crossroad, 1990; first published in French, 1989), p. 12.

25. Denis Baly, *God and History in the Old Testament* (New York: Harper & Row, 1976), p. 36, n. 13.

CHAPTER 2

THINKING ABOUT GOD: WHY PANENTHEISM?

God is the beyond in our midst.[1]

Panentheism as a way of thinking about God affirms both the transcendence of God and the immanence of God. For panentheism, God is not a being "out there." The Greek roots of the word point to its meaning: *pan* means "everything," *en* means "in," and *theos* means "God." Panentheism thus means "everything is *in* God." God is more than everything (and thus transcendent), yet everything is in God (hence God is immanent). For panentheism, God is "right here," even as God is also more than "right here."[2]

Panentheism is very different from pantheism, with which it is often confused. Pantheism lacks the extra syllable *en,* which makes all the difference. Pantheism (without the *en*) identifies the universe with God: God and the universe are coextensive (literally, "everything is God"). Pantheism affirms only God's immanence and essentially denies God's transcendence; though the sacred is present in everything, it is not more than everything.[3] But pan*en*theism affirms both transcendence (God's otherness or moreness) and immanence (God's presence). God is not to be identified with the sum total of things. Rather, God is more than everything, even as God is present everywhere. God is all around us and within us, and we are within God.

Panentheism as a root concept for thinking about God is a broad umbrella that encompasses a variety of more specific theological positions. Within it I include all concepts of the sacred that strongly affirm both the transcendence and immanence of God. It is what John Macquarrie calls "dialectical theism": the affirmation of two apparent opposites, God as "beyond" and God as "right here."[4] God is more than the world (and more than a metaphor for the world). Yet God is present in the world—not only (or at all?) in moments of supernatural intervention (the God "out there" momentarily breaking into the world), but always "here," and in moments disclosed to us.

Panentheism is unfamiliar to many Christians, so deeply entrenched is supernatural theism. When they do hear of it, some welcome it enthusiastically because it makes sense and fits their own experience. Others dismiss it as foreign to the Christian tradition, often because they confuse it with pantheism. When this confusion occurs, the only two options for thinking about God are supernatural theism or pantheism. Because the orthodox Christian tradition is not pantheistic, it follows that supernatural theism must be the Christian option.[5] But panentheism is not only a third option, different from both supernatural theism and pantheism; it is also, as I shall report later in this chapter, deeply rooted in the Christian tradition. Indeed, panentheism—because it affirms both the transcendence and immanence of God—seems to me to be the orthodox Christian root concept of God, even though the notion is not widely known in popular Christianity.

But why should we think this way? Why should we think of God with a panentheistic root concept? Why should we think of God as "right here" rather than out there? When I first ran into this way of conceptualizing God in modern thinkers like Tillich and Robinson, it seemed to me like a way of trying to evade the intellectual difficulties posed by thinking of God as a being "out there"—a defensive position and a retreat from robust belief in God.

But I now see this as one of the virtues of panentheism: it does genuinely resolve much of the intellectual difficulty posed by supernatural theism. For the most part, modern skepticism and atheism are a rejection of supernatural theism, but if God is not thought of as a supernatural being separate from the universe, then the persuasive force of much of modern atheism vanishes. The resolution of this intellectual difficulty about God is no small matter, for it means that the "God question" becomes an open rather than a closed one.

In addition, there are two more reasons for taking panentheism seriously as an alternative Christian root concept for thinking about God: it is biblical, and certain kinds of religious experience point to this way of thinking about God.

GOD "RIGHT HERE": PANENTHEISM IN THE BIBLE

As already noted, the Bible more often than not speaks of God as if God were a being "out there." This is the natural language of devotion and worship: because of the personal nature of the relationship with God, it is natural to personify God. There is nothing wrong with this language, unless, through literalization, it becomes an intellectual and spiritual obstacle.

But the Bible also speaks of God as "right here" and not simply "out there." It does so in many ways. There are both themes and texts pointing to panentheism.

Both the Hebrew Bible and the Christian Testament speak of "the glory of God," which the Jewish theologian Abraham Heschel defines as "the effulgence of a living presence."[6] The glory of God is the radiance of God's presence, and the earth is filled with it. The six-winged creatures around the throne of God in Isaiah's great vision exclaim, "The whole earth is full of God's glory."[7] Similarly, Ezekiel sees "the earth shining with God's glory."[8] The author of Psalm 19 sees it in the night sky: "The heavens declare the glory of God."

Psalm 29 describes the glory of God as experienced in the awesome power of a thunderstorm sweeping in from the Mediterranean and moving down the land from Lebanon in the north to Kadesh in the south:

> The voice of the LORD is over the waters;
> the God of glory thunders,
> the LORD, over mighty waters. . . .
> The voice of the LORD breaks the cedars;
> the LORD breaks the cedars of Lebanon. . . .
> The voice of the LORD flashes forth flames of fire.
> The voice of the LORD shakes the wilderness . . . of Kadesh.
> The voice of the LORD causes the oaks to whirl,

and strips the forests bare;
and in God's temple, all say, "Glory!"

Not only nature but people can reflect or be filled with the glory of God. Moses experienced the glory of God on Mount Sinai, and according to the story in the book of Exodus, his face continued to glow afterward.⁹ In the New Testament, the author of John's gospel and Paul both speak of Jesus as filled with the glory of God:

And we have seen his glory, the glory as of a father's only son, full of grace and truth.¹⁰

For it is the God who said, "Let light shine out of darkness," who has shone in our hearts to give the light of the knowledge of the glory of God in the face of Jesus Christ.¹¹

Thus, according to the Bible, the glory of God—the presence of God—is not simply somewhere else but "right here," known and experienced in this world.

The Bible affirms the presence of God in other ways as well. One of the names of God in the Hebrew Bible points to God's presence. In the famous story of the call of Moses, Moses asks God, "What is your name?" In Hebrew, God's response is *ehyeh asher ehyeh,* a difficult phrase that is most commonly translated into English as "I am who I am."¹² But Martin Buber, the best known Jewish religious scholar of this century, argues persuasively that the Hebrew verb *ehyeh* means "being there, being present" and that the phrase as a whole should be translated, "I will be present as I will be present."¹³ God's name suggests that God is the presence "who is present in every now and every here."¹⁴

The theme of God's presence is beautifully expressed in words addressed to the Jewish people in exile in Babylon in the sixth century B.C.E.: "Do not be afraid, for *I am with you.*"¹⁵ In the New Testament, Jesus is named as the presence of God; in Matthew's birth story, Joseph is told to name him "Immanuel," a Hebrew word that means "God with us."¹⁶

The Bible also speaks of God as the encompassing Spirit, as a reality all around us. Panentheism is implicit in Psalm 139:

You have searched me and known me;
    you know when I sit down and when I rise up. . . .

> You go before me and behind me,
>   and lay your hand upon me. . . .
> Where can I go from your Spirit?
>   Or where can I flee from your presence?
> If I ascend to heaven, you are there;
>   if I make my bed in Sheol, you are there.
> If I take the wings of the morning and settle
>   at the farthest limits of the sea,
>   even there your hand shall lead me,
>   and your right hand shall hold me fast.

The author imagines journeying through the whole of reality, the three-story universe of heaven, earth, and Sheol, and to the farthest limits of the sea. The affirmation is striking: no matter where I go, God is there. How can that be? Because everything is in God. There is no place where I can be outside God's presence.

In a speech attributed to him by the author of Acts, the apostle Paul spoke in the marketplace of Athens about the human quest for God and affirmed that God is not far away but near—indeed, here:

> They would search for God and perhaps grope for God and find God—though indeed God is not far from each one of us. For "In God we live and move and have our being."[17]

According to this text, where are we in relation to God? We are in God: we live and move and have our being in God. God is not only "up in heaven" but "right here," as the encompassing Spirit all around us, in whom we are.

A number of biblical texts speak of *knowing* God. This does not mean knowing *about* God but a direct knowing like that experienced between lovers. Indeed, sometimes the word for sexual intercourse is used to speak of knowing God. Abraham Heschel in particular has noted how central this usage is in the prophet Hosea. Hosea indicted his hearers for *not* knowing God. Obviously, they knew *about* God and indeed worshiped God; what they lacked (and needed) was intimate direct knowing of God, like lover and beloved.[18]

Though the author of the book of Job uses the language of seeing rather than knowing, he clearly speaks of direct experience of God rather than beliefs about God. In the climactic exchange between God and Job at the close of the book, Job says, "I had heard of you with the hearing of the ear, but now my eye sees you."[19] The New Testament also speaks of knowing God. The author of John's gospel wrote, "This is eternal life: *to know* God."[20] According to the verse, eternal life is a present reality, not simply a future one, and the content of eternal life is the experience of knowing God in the present. If God can be "seen" and "known," then God is accessible to human experience and cannot simply be transcendent but must also be thought of as here.

Moreover, knowing God is attested to not only by biblical texts explicitly referring to it but in the experience of the central figures of the biblical tradition. The stories about Moses' experiences of the sacred, the call stories of the prophets, and the story of Jesus all speak of people who *knew* the sacred. For them, the sacred was an element of experience, not simply an article of belief.

EXPERIENCES OF THE SACRED

This leads to the second primary reason for thinking about God with a panentheistic model. Namely, there are particular kinds of experiences that seem to those who have them to be experiences of the sacred. To state the obvious conclusion: if the sacred—if God—can be experienced, then God is not simply somewhere else but also right here.

The most dramatic of these experiences involve nonordinary states of consciousness. They are "ecstatic," which means literally to be out of oneself, or out of one's ordinary state of consciousness. Sometimes occurring spontaneously, these nonordinary states can also be entered through ritualized means and spiritual disciplines.

Ecstatic religious experiences and their implications for how we see reality have been made central by many scholars of religion, classically by William James and Rudolf Otto near the beginning of this century and more recently by Mircea Eliade and Huston Smith.[21] Otto spoke of them as experiences of "the numinous." Eliade spoke of them as "hierophanies" (manifestations of the sacred) and "theophanies" (manifestations of the sacred as God).

In the nonordinary states of consciousness that mark these experiences, reality is experienced as "more" than the visible world of our ordinary consciousness. Importantly, the experiences have a noetic quality to them—that is, people who have them consistently say that they involve a *knowing* (and not simply a feeling).[22] They involve a vivid experiential sense of seeing or encountering or becoming aware of another layer or kind of reality. Various terms are used for this other layer of reality: an alternate reality, the numinous, the sacred, a world of spirit.

Such experiences have occurred across cultures and throughout history. The founders of most of the major religions are reported to have had such experiences; examples include the theophanies of Moses at the burning bush and on Mount Sinai, the enlightenment experience of the Buddha, the baptismal and wilderness visions of Jesus, and the visions of Muhammad. But ordinary people also have them.[23]

Though sharp distinctions are difficult to draw, a categorization into types of experiences of the sacred illustrates their variety. Moreover, one or more of these kinds of experience may connect to our experience. Because these experiences stretch (and even shatter) modern notions of what is real and what is possible, I invite you to suspend for a moment whatever skepticism you may have.[24]

Visions are vivid experiences of momentarily seeing into another layer or level of reality. Like a dream, they involve visual images, though they can also include photisms (experiences of light) and auditions (sounds, especially voices). Known in all societies, visions are more common than we in the modern world might suppose.[25]

Sometimes visions are of God, or otherworldly beings, or bizarre creatures not found in the world of our ordinary experience. Isaiah saw seraphim—six-winged creatures—around the throne of God; Daniel saw creatures like a lion with an eagle's wings, a bear with three tusks, a leopard with four wings and four heads, another with ten horns.[26] Sometimes visions are of natural or cultural objects, as in Jeremiah's visions of an almond tree and a boiling pot or Amos's vision of locusts devouring the crops.[27] But whether the content is God, strange creatures, or "ordinary" objects (or some combination of all of these), visions have a numinous quality—a sense of the sacred and a sense that they come from God.

Felicitas Goodman, a contemporary anthropologist specializing in the study of visions, argues that visions are to be distinguished from hallucinations, which are delusions in which nothing real corresponds to what is reported.[28] In a vision, "the quality of the experience suggests that the content of the perception is *real,* a direct, unmediated contact with *a nonordinary aspect of reality* that is external and independent of the perceiver."[29] Visions point to an alternate reality, a layer of reality other than (and alongside of) the world of our ordinary experience.

In visions, God is typically experienced as a reality separate from the person—either because the vision involves "seeing" God or because the vision seems given by God. But even though God is experienced as an "other" (and thus as transcendent), the point remains that in a vision the sacred is accessible to experience and is therefore also present (immanent).

Shamanic experiences are similar in one respect to visions and may be regarded as a special type of visionary experience.[30] In them, the person not only sees into another level of reality but journeys into it, embarking on "magical flights" and "spirit journeys."[31] Shamans enter the alternate reality and interact with it for the sake of their people. They are technicians of the sacred; they have techniques for entering the alternate reality and techniques for mediating, on behalf of the group, spiritual power (often healing power but also divination and clairvoyance, among other functions). Sometimes shamans seek to affect entities encountered in the alternate reality. There are also reports of journeying through alternate reality to another place in ordinary reality; there the shamans are able to see events that are happening at a great distance from their actual physical location.

Mystical experiences involve ecstatic states of consciousness in which one is vividly aware of the presence of God. The contemporary Catholic scholar Bernard McGinn defines "the mystical element in Christianity" as "that part of its belief and practices that concerns the preparation for, the consciousness of, and the reaction to what can be described as *the immediate or direct presence of God.*"[32]

Earlier in this century, Rufus Jones, a Quaker scholar, defined mysticism as

> a type of religion which puts the emphasis on immediate awareness of relation with God, on direct and intimate consciousness of the Divine Presence. It is religion in its most acute, intense, and living stage.[33]

About the same time, Anglican theologian William Ralph Inge, dean of Saint Paul's Cathedral in London, defined it as "the attempt to realize, in thought and feeling, the immanence of the temporal in the eternal, and of the eternal in the temporal."[34] Though mysticism has not been well regarded by much of modern Protestant theology, it is a central element in the history of religious experience, including the Christian tradition.[35]

Mystical experiences have been divided into two major types.[36] *Extravertive mystical experiences* are "eyes open" mystical experiences. These are moments when one sees the same world one would otherwise see, but it looks radically different. One sees the world "filled with the glory of God." A landscape is transformed and suffused with light, as if illuminated from within or behind. Bushes burn without being consumed, aflame with divine radiance. The world may look new, fresh, wondrous. In Abraham Heschel's phrase, these are moments of "radical amazement" when the categories and language with which we domesticate reality momentarily fall away and we experience "the world in its grandeur" as "full of a spiritual radiance, for which we have neither name nor concept."[37]

In such moments, to use sacramental language, the sacred is experienced "in, with, and under" the world of ordinary experience, even though in moments or minutes of extravertive mystical experience, that world is not experienced as "ordinary." The temporal is experienced in the eternal and the eternal in the temporal, to use Dean Inge's language. Such experiences are typically accompanied by a change in one's sense of oneself. The boundary between self and world that marks our ordinary consciousness becomes soft, and one is aware more of a sense of connectedness than of separation.[38]

Introvertive mystical experiences are "eyes closed" mystical experiences. Typically occurring during deep meditation, there is a sense of entering the presence of God or even becoming absorbed into God. Metaphors of both depth and height are used to speak of the experience: one may descend to a deep layer of the self or psyche where the self opens out into a sea of being experienced as God or the God beyond God; alternatively, the soul may experience itself ascending to God. Mystics speak of both kataphatic and apophatic experiences; the former involve images, the latter do not. As in extraverted mystical experiences, the boundary of the self becomes very soft and may even disappear so that one experiences communion or union with the sacred.

Dreams sometimes mediate a sense of the sacred. Not all dreams do; indeed, most do not. But two aspects of dreams are relevant. First, some dreams have a numinous quality to them in which the dream itself conveys a sense of the presence of the sacred. Second, the interpretation of dreams (especially within a Jungian framework) often suggests that there is a wisdom in them. In particular, it sometimes seems that dreams put us in touch with an internal wisdom that knows more about us than we know about ourselves. This source of internal wisdom is called by the contemporary Jungian scholar E. F. Edinger "the Self" (with a capital *S*) and is viewed as equivalent to God.[39] If we combine this with the notion of God's omnipresence, it leads to a concept of God as *that within us, within which we also are.*

Near-death experiences seem to those who have them to be experiences of the sacred. They are reported by many people who experience a near-death state. The experiences themselves are remarkable, combining visionary elements and an out-of-body experience, and have relatively constant elements across time and cultures. They include a sense of journeying through a tunnel, leaving one's body, and encountering a being of light.[40]

It is important to note that in addition to these ecstatic types of religious experience, there are less dramatic experiences in which people report an *awareness of God's presence.* These do not involve visions or transformed landscapes or deep mystical union or beings of light but nevertheless seem to persons who have them to be experiences of divine presence. Though quite ordinary compared to the extraordinary character of ecstatic experiences, they stand out in the memory of the individual as remarkable.[41] The following are just a few examples of experiencing what might be called "the dailiness of God":

- A husband weeping in a hotel room about the impending dissolution of his marriage and seeing his own responsibility for it becomes aware of God's presence and a voice saying, "You are forgiven," and experiences a lightness of being and release from anguish.

- A woman conducting a funeral service for a homeless man who had been stabbed, the service attended only by other homeless men who did not know the victim, experiences the room suffused by a golden light that feels like the presence of God.

- A man sitting on a stump in a forest, thinking about his life, experiences a still and accepting presence around him that seems unmistakably to be God.

- A woman receiving the bread and wine of the Eucharist regularly experiences it as Christ becoming present to her.

One of the finest conceptual expressions of how the sacred is experienced in the everyday is Martin Buber's description of I-It and I-You ways of being in his famous book *I and Thou.*[42] Buber argues that we as humans have two fundamentally different ways of being in relationship to the world (by which he means the totality of things, including nature, culture, and persons): the way of I–It and the way of I–You.

The way of I–It is by far the most common; in fact, it represents normal adult consciousness. Within this mode of being, the world is experienced within the framework of the subject–object distinction: "I" experience myself as a subject separate from a world of objects, as an ego aware of itself and its differentiation from the world. Even our grammar embodies this difference: I (subject) see you (object). The I–It way of being is the world of our ordinary experience: the world of cause and effect, of ordered space and time; the world as domesticated by the culturally created grid of language, categories, and knowledge.

I–You moments are very different, much harder to describe, and comparatively rare. I–You moments "appear as queer lyric-dramatic episodes" and are often dismissed by people for whom the I–It world seems to be the real world.[43] "How powerful is the continuum of the It-world," Buber writes, "and how tender the manifestations of the You!"[44]

The I–You way of being is the opposite of I–It. It is the world of relation and connectedness as opposed to separation and differentiation. The world within an I–You mode of being is uncategorized and thus appears fresh, new, and undomesticated. The "I" of I–You moments is also different from the "I" of I–It experience: the "I" of I–You is wholly present and wholly involved so that no part of the self is left over. The self-conscious I (the ego aware of being an I and able to be a spectator even of itself) disappears; ego boundaries and ego awareness momentarily melt away.[45] Thus the world of I–You is the world of no-time and of the eternal now, for there is no part of the self that is thinking about past or future.

In I–You moments, the world is known as a "You"—that is, as the phrase itself implies, as a presence rather than as an object. Indeed, such moments are glimpses of "the eternal You," experiences of the sacred in which the beyond is experienced in the finite and in the here and now.

At a celebration of his eightieth birthday, Buber denied being a prophet, philosopher, or theologian but instead said about himself, "I am only someone who has seen something and who goes to a window and points."[46] What he points to is "the eternal You," known in the midst of the everyday.

Thus far I have stressed the cognitive aspect of experiences of the sacred. As noted earlier, according to those who have them, they involve knowing and not just feeling. I now wish to emphasize the affective ("feeling") aspect of these experiences and their effects. They are commonly marked by joy, bliss, and peace.[47] Moreover, they frequently lead to a transformed and loving perception of people and the world. Some examples combining these elements will help to flesh out this section on experiences of the sacred.

Though extravertive mystical experiences are frequently spoken of as nature mysticism, the Irish poet William Butler Yeats describes an experience of the sacred that happened to him in a London coffee shop. In part four of his poem "Vacillation," the first five lines describe the setting and the last four the experience:

> My fiftieth year had come and gone,
> I sat, a solitary man, in a crowded London shop,
> An open book and empty cup
> On the marble table top.
> While on the shop and street I gazed,
> My body of a sudden blazed;
> And twenty minutes more or less
> It seemed, so great my happiness,
> That I was blessed and could bless.

Yeats speaks of a happiness "so great" that he "was blessed and could bless."

The Hindu poet Rabindranath Tagore writes of an experience combining transformed cognition and joy:

> I suddenly felt as if some ancient mist had in a moment lifted from my sight and the ultimate significance of all things was laid bare. . . . Immediately I found the world bathed in a wonderful radiance with waves of beauty and joy swelling on every side, and no person or thing in the world seemed to me trivial or unpleasing.[48]

Joy is central to an ecstatic experience that the French mathematician and philosopher Blaise Pascal had over three hundred years ago:

> In the year of grace 1654, Monday 23 November . . . from about half-past ten in the evening till about half an hour after midnight:
> FIRE
> God of Abraham, God of Isaac, God of Jacob. Not of the philosophers and the learned. Certitude. Certitude. Emotion. Joy . . . Joy! Joy! Joy! Tears of Joy . . . My God . . . let me not be separated from thee for ever.

Pascal carried this description of his experience under a drawing of a blazing cross with him the rest of his life, perhaps suggesting that what he had seen was a cross that (like Moses' experience at the bush) burned without being consumed. The description was found on his body when he died.

Another example of ecstatic joy and transformed perception comes from Billy Bray in the nineteenth century, whom William James describes as "an excellent little illiterate English evangelist":

> In an instant the Lord made me so happy that I cannot express what I felt. I shouted for joy. I praised God with my whole heart. . . . Everything looked new to me, the people, the fields, the cattle, the trees. I was like a new man in a new world. I can't help praising the Lord. As I go along the street, I lift up one foot, and it seems to say "Glory"; and I lift up the other, and it seems to say "Amen"; and so they keep up like that all the time I am walking.[49]

Finally, Leslie Weatherhead, a British theologian and clergyman from earlier in this century, describes a mystical experience that made him certain of the reality of God. It happened on a "murky November Saturday evening" in a third-class compartment on a train leaving London:

> For a few seconds only, I suppose, the whole compartment was filled with light. This is the only way I know in which to describe the moment, for there was nothing to *see* at all. I felt caught up into some tremendous sense of being within a loving, triumphant and shining purpose. I never felt more humble. I never felt more exalted. A most curious, but overwhelming sense possessed me and filled me with ecstasy. . . . All men were shining and glorious beings who in the end would enter incredible joy. . . . An indescribable joy possessed me. All this happened over fifty years ago but even now I can see myself in the corner of that dingy third-class compartment with the feeble lights of inverted gas mantles overhead and the Vauxhall Station platform outside with milk cans standing there. In a few moments the glory departed—all but one curious, lingering feeling. I loved everybody in that compartment. It sounds silly now, and indeed I blush to write it, but at that moment I think I would have died for any one of the people in that compartment.[50]

IMPLICATIONS FOR OUR THINKING ABOUT GOD

If we take experiences of the sacred as the starting point for our thinking about God, they have a number of implications.

First, it seems to me that ecstatic religious experience is the primary reason for taking seriously the reality of the sacred, of God. These experiences lead to the inference that there is more than one kind of reality, more than one level of reality, and that these other levels or layers can be (and are) known.

Of course, such experiences do not *prove* the reality of God or the sacred. Such a demonstration is impossible. But I find the evidential value of religious experience to be far more interesting and suggestive than the traditional "proofs" of God's existence, which I am convinced do not work. The varieties of religious experience suggest that the sacred —God—is an element of experience, not simply an article of faith to be believed in.

To put this point differently, experiences like these rupture "Flatland." *Flatland* is the title and central image of a book written late in the nineteenth century, allegedly by an author named (appropriately) "A Square" but in fact by an Anglican headmaster and scholar named Edwin A. Abbott.[51] Flatland is a two-dimensional universe having only length and width (and thus lacking height or depth), a plane inhabited by two-dimensional creatures—squares, triangles, rectangles, and so forth.

The author invites us to imagine Flatland being intersected by a sphere and what the Flatlanders would experience as the sphere passed through it. They would see a point as the sphere first touched the horizontal plane of Flatland, then an expanding circle until the sphere was halfway through, then a contracting circle diminishing to a point and finally vanishing.

What kinds of explanations might the Flatlanders have for what had happened? Possibly many—but they would have no chance at all of understanding what had really happened so long as they tried to do so within the framework of a two-dimensional understanding of reality.

Flatland is obviously an image for the modern worldview, the materialistic and mechanistic image of reality that emerged during the Enlightenment. Though the modern worldview, of course, knows three dimensions, there is a sense in which it is a "flat" worldview—that what is real is the visible material world of our ordinary experience. Experiences of the sacred shatter Flatland. Visions happen, enlightenment experiences happen, paranormal experiences happen. These experiences suggest that reality is far more mysterious than any and all of our domestications—whether scientific or religious—make it out to be.

They suggest that reality is more, much more, than modernity has imagined.

Abraham Heschel describes well the relationship between the immediate and preconceptual awareness of God's presence and all of our conceptual statements about God:

> The certainty of the realness of God does not come about as a corollary of logical premises, as a leap from the realm of logic to the realm of ontology, from an assumption to a fact. It is, on the contrary, a transition from an immediate apprehension to a thought, from a preconceptual awareness to a definite assurance, from being overwhelmed by the presence of God to an awareness of God's existence.

Then he adds, provocatively, "The truth . . . is that to say 'God is' means less than what our immediate awareness contains. *The statement 'God is' is an understatement.*"[52] Of course, Heschel does not mean that the statement "God is" is wrong; rather, he points to the priority of experience of the sacred over all conceptualizations.[53]

Second, these experiences should affect how we think of God in relationship to the world. To state the conclusion that I announced earlier, if God can be experienced, then God is right here, all around us. The religious experiences of humankind in general and of the biblical and Christian traditions in particular suggest that we must think of God as both immanent and transcendent.

In short, these experiences point to what I have spoken of as a panentheistic model of God. Not only can such a model take religious experience seriously but it is also faithful to the Christian tradition, which affirms both the immanence and transcendence of God. Moreover, it is intellectually more adequate than supernatural theism's concept of God as wholly transcendent; it does not have the difficulties associated with thinking of God as "out there."

Affirming both the immanence and transcendence of God affects the meaning of transcendence. It becomes something other than the spatial imaginings of my youth, when I thought it meant that God was elsewhere, out there and not here. Rather, the transcendence of God refers to the mystery and ineffability of the sacred, to God as surpassingly more and surpassingly other than the world of our ordinary experience, even as God is also immanent and sometimes experienced. God is the "beyond in our midst," as the German theologian and martyr Dietrich Bonhoeffer put it in the last year of his life in a Nazi prison cell.[54]

The affirmation of God's presence runs throughout the Christian tradition. One of the most famous and powerful statements comes from Saint Augustine about 1,600 years ago. Reflecting on what seems to have been an introvertive mystical experience and addressing God as "You," Augustine wrote:[55]

> How late I came to love you, O Beauty so ancient and so fresh, how late I came to love you! *You were within me,* yet I had gone outside to seek you. Unlovely myself, I rushed toward all those lovely things you had made. *And always you were with me,* I was not with you. All these beauties kept me far from you—although they would not have existed at all unless *they had their being in you.* You called, you cried, you shattered my deafness. You sparkled, you blazed, you drove away my blindness. You shed your fragrance, and I drew in my breath and I pant for you. *I tasted* and now I hunger and thirst. *You touched me,* and now I burn with longing for your peace.[56]

"I was outside. You were within." Such was his experience. Yet for Augustine, God was not simply within. Rather, "God is always present to us and to all things; it is that we, like blind persons, do not have the eyes to see" God.[57]

It is the same point made in this century by the Catholic monk Thomas Merton:

> Life is this simple. We are living in a world that is absolutely transparent, and God is shining through it all the time. This is not just a fable or a nice story. It is true. If we abandon ourselves to God and forget ourselves, we see it sometimes, and we see it maybe frequently. God shows Himself everywhere, in everything—in people and in things and in nature and in events. It becomes very obvious that God is everywhere and in everything and we cannot be without Him. It's impossible. The only thing is that we don't see it.[58]

The sense of God's presence in everything has frequently been expressed by poets. Elizabeth Barrett Browning wrote:

> Earth's crammed with heaven
> And every common bush alive with God.
> Only he who sees takes off his shoes;
> The rest sit around and pluck blackberries.[59]

In *Tintern Abbey,* William Wordsworth wrote:

> And I have felt
> A presence that disturbs me with the joy
> Of elevated thoughts; a sense sublime
> Of something far more deeply interfused,
> Whose dwelling is the light of setting suns,
> And the round ocean and the living air,
> And the blue sky, and in the mind of man,
> A motion and a spirit that impels
> All thinking things, all objects of all thought,
> And rolls through all things.[60]

Yet though panentheism seems to me to be the most adequate model of God, we must also beware of all conceptualizations of God. The transcendence of God means in part that God is ineffable. Over 2,500 years ago, Lao-tzu, a Chinese philosopher and mystic widely regarded as the founder of Taoism, whose Western influence is increasingly profound both in the adoption of Taoist perspectives and in the impact of Taoist-inspired Zen Buddhism, said, "The Tao that can be named is not the eternal Tao." The Tao (pronounced *dow*) is Lao-tzu's term for the formless nonmaterial reality that is the source of all things without itself being a thing, as well as the way of life lived in accord with such a reality. Yet if one can conceptualize it, one is no longer talking about it.

In the Christian tradition, Augustine similarly said:

> Before experiencing God you thought you could talk about God; when you begin to experience God you realize that what you are experiencing you cannot put into words.[61]

In the Jewish tradition, the prohibition against graven images of God makes the same point. It is not simply that one should not make a statue or physical image of God. Rather it means that God is beyond all images, physical and mental. Martin Buber's understanding of the origin of the divine name *Yahweh* is suggestive. Buber argues that it originated in an exclamation drawn forth by ecstatic religious experience and means roughly, "O the One!"[62] The most sacred name of God is an exclamation uttered in a moment of religious ecstasy. God cannot be named, only exclaimed.

Stephen Mitchell, a contemporary Buddhist translator who comes out of the Jewish tradition, has created a parable that expresses the ineffability of God:

Everyone knows what happened at the bottom of Mount Sinai, but no one mentions what happened on the top. In a way, this is unavoidable: the eye can't see itself, the equation can't prove itself. Nevertheless, a few of our sages have spoken. (In order to say anything, they had to be there.)

Rabbi Levi said, "On the top of Mount Sinai, Moses was given the choice of receiving the commandments or seeing God face to face. He knew that he could not see God without first dying. It was like looking into a mirror with no reflection inside."

Rabbi Ezra said, "Moses did receive a commandment, but only one, only the First. All the others blended into silence, as all colors blend into white."

Rabbi Gamaliel said, "Moses received only the first phrase of the First Commandment: I am the Unnamable."

Rabbi Elhanan said, "Moses saw on Sinai what he had heard from the Burning Bush. There was just one message: I am."

Rabbi Samuel said, "Not even that. The only word the Unnamable whispered was *I.*"

Rabbi Yosi said, "In the holy tongue, *I* is *anokhi: aleph-nun-kaph-yod*. What Moses received from God was the first letter of *I.*"

But *aleph* is a silent letter.

Rabbi Yosi said, "Just so."[63]

All of our thinking about God—our concepts, as well as our images, which we shall consider in the next chapter—are attempts to express the ineffable. The ineffable—one in whom we live and move and have our being—is beyond all of our concepts, even this one.

And yet the ineffable, the sacred, is real and present. To use an inscription important to Carl Jung, "Bidden or not bidden, God is present." These words were carved in Latin over Jung's front door as a reminder to both him and his patients. They are also on Jung's tombstone. God is surpassingly more than our words can express, yet God is "right here."

To illustrate this claim with a story: a couple of years ago, I overheard a meeting of the worship committee in an Episcopal church. They were talking about the need to introduce more inclusive language into the

Sunday services. All agreed that the exclusive use of male pronouns for God needed to be changed, but they were perplexed about how to do it. Suggestions to replace "he" with "she" or to alternate "he" and "she" were rejected as inappropriate or awkward. Then someone said, "Well, whatever we do, we can't use 'it,' for whatever God is, God is not an 'it.'" A thought suddenly occurred to me: the problem isn't really whether to use "he," "she," or "it"; rather, the problem is using third-person language for God. When do we use third-person language to talk about somebody? When she or he isn't there. Third-person language implies absence. But if we take seriously that God is present, the most appropriate language for God is second-person language—God as "You." God is "the you" in our midst, who knows us already and who yearns to be known by us.[64]

Buber speaks powerfully of the inadequacy of all of our concepts and images of God even as he underlines that God as "You" speaks to us. What matters is not how we speak of God but that we hear God's voice:

> Time after time, the images must be broken, the iconoclasts ["smashers of images"] must have their way. For the iconoclast is the soul in us which rebels against having an image that can no longer be believed in, elevated above our heads as a thing that demands to be worshipped. In longing for a god, we try again and again to set up a greater, a more genuine and more just image, which is intended to be more glorious than the last and only proves the more unsatisfactory. The commandment, "Thou shalt not make unto thee an image," does not, of course, refer merely to sculptured or painted images, but to our fantasy, to all the power of our imagination as well. But we are forced time and again to make images, and forced to destroy them when we realize that we have not succeeded. The images topple, but the voice is never silenced. . . . The voice speaks in the guise of everything that happens, in the guise of all world events; it speaks to all generations, makes demands upon us, and summons us to accept responsibility. . . . It is of the utmost importance not to lose one's openness. But to be open means not to shut out the voice—call it what you will. It does not matter what you call it. All that matters is that you hear it.[65]

Though our images and concepts of God are not sacred in themselves and are subject to change, it matters whether we conceptualize God in the third person, as a distant being who is not here. This way of thinking about God, which many of us learned as children, does make God seem unreal, remote, distant, and problematic. The way sketched in this chapter, I am convinced, makes God seem real and near.

Moreover, thinking about God as both transcendent and immanent, as the beyond who is "right here," leads to a quite different image of the Christian life from the one that dominated the early decades of my life. I now see that the Christian life is not essentially about beliefs and requirements; it is not about believing in a God "out there" for the sake of an afterlife later. Rather, thinking about God panentheistically leads to a relational understanding of the Christian life, which is, I am convinced, both true and profoundly life-giving.

Put very simply and directly, the course of my own Christian journey from supernatural theism to panentheism has led me, experientially and intellectually, to three central convictions:

God is real.

The Christian life is about entering into a relationship with God as known in Jesus Christ.

That relationship can—and will—change your life.

Notes

1. Dietrich Bonhoeffer, *Letters and Papers from Prison,* enlarged edition, ed. Eberhard Bethge (New York: Macmillan, 1972), p. 282.

2. I sometimes seek to explain the difference between supernatural theism and panentheism by inviting my students to imagine how one might diagram God in relationship to the universe. I suggest representing the universe with an oval. Where is God in relationship to the universe? Supernatural theism thinks of God as a being outside the oval; God and the universe are spatially separate. Panentheism would represent God as a larger oval that includes the oval of the universe; God encompasses the universe, and the universe is in God. Of course, these diagrams cannot be taken literally. It does not make sense to think of either the universe or God as having borders, as the ovals suggest.

3. Paul Tillich cautions against a too simplistic reading of pantheism; see his *Systematic Theology,* vol. 1 (Chicago: University of Chicago Press, 1951), pp. 233–34. Beyond my strong emphasis that pantheism and panentheism are very different, pantheism is not important to me in this book, so I have not concerned myself with refinements.

4. See Chapter One above, n. 2. As I use the term, panentheism includes all forms of dialectical theism, including theological positions as diverse as process theology, Huston Smith's "primordial tradition," Tillich's understanding of God as "the ground of being," and (as I will argue later in this chapter) major voices within the biblical and Christian theological traditions. One may thus speak of a process panentheism, a primordial panentheism, a Tillichian panentheism, and so forth.

5. Even theologically trained people can make this mistake. For example, see Ben Witherington III, *The Jesus Quest* (Downers Grove, IL: Intervarsity, 1995), an analysis of contemporary Jesus scholarship from a conservative-evangelical perspective. On p. 106, commenting about what I say about God in *Meeting Jesus Again for the First Time,* he says: "More disturbing" is "what Borg says about the nature of God," which "sounds altogether very similar to what we hear from modern advocates of New Age philosophy. God as a power or force or source of energy that suffuses all things is substituted for God the personal and transcendent Being who created the universe and all that is in it." Witherington apparently does not take seriously that I affirm both the

transcendence and immanence of God, and the appropriateness of addressing God as "you" (as a presence, and not simply an energy); moreover, he seems to think that affirming the immanence of God is akin to "New Age" thought (and therefore questionable). He seems not to see that panentheism is a Christian option quite different from pantheism.

6. Abraham Heschel, *God in Search of Man: A Philosophy of Judaism* (New York: Noonday Press, 1955), pp. 80–87; quotation from p. 83.

7. Isa. 6.3.

8. Ezek. 43.2.

9. Exod. 33.18–23, 34.29–35.

10. John 1.14.

11. 2 Cor. 4.6.

12. Exod. 3.14 (the whole story is found in 3.1–15).

13. Martin Buber, *Moses: The Revelation and the Covenant* (New York: Harper & Row, 1958), p. 52.

14. Maurice S. Friedman, *Martin Buber: The Life of Dialogue* (New York: Harper & Row, 1960), p. 246.

15. Isa. 43.5.

16. Matt. 1.23. The final verse of Matthew's gospel returns to the theme: the risen Christ promises his followers, "I am with you always, to the end of the age" (Matt. 28.20).

17. Acts 17.27–28. Though the quotation is sometimes attributed to a Greek philosopher named Epimenides, the author of Acts in effect baptizes it by putting it in the mouth of Paul; he obviously thought it was an appropriate way for Paul to speak of God.

18. Heschel, *The Prophets*, vol. 1 (New York; Harper & Row, 1969), pp. 57–60. For negative and positive examples, see Hos. 4.1 ("there is no knowledge of God in the land") and 6.6 (God desires "knowledge of God rather than burnt offerings"). See also Robert Dentan, *The Knowledge of God in Ancient Israel* (New York: Seabury Press, 1968), pp. 38–39.

19. Job 42.5.

20. John 17.3.

21. James, *The Varieties of Religious Experience;* Rudolf Otto, *The Idea of the Holy,* trans. John Harvey (New York: Oxford University Press, 1958; first published in 1917); Mircea Elíade, *The Sacred and the Profane,* trans. Willard Trask (New York: Harcourt Brace Jovanovich, 1959); Smith, *Forgotten Truth.*

22. For "noetic" as a characteristic of these experiences, see James, *The Varieties of Religious Experience.* See also Andrew Greeley, *Ecstasy: A Way of Knowing* (Englewood Cliffs, NJ: Prentice Hall, 1974). The title of his book makes the point. See also his comments on p. 4: according to the mystics themselves, "the experience is more one of *knowing* than of feeling." What is heightened in the experience are "the cognitive faculties"; the mystics now "know something others do not know and that they did not know before." "The mystic *knows* that cognition is at the core" of the experience.

23. Greeley, *Ecstasy,* p. 11: there is evidence that about half of the American population report having had at least one experience "of union with 'a powerful spiritual force that draws me out of myself.' "

24. David Griffin, *God and Religion in the Postmodern World,* pp. 55–56, correctly observes that the modern worldview denies the possibility of an experience of God.

25. Of the first three thousand accounts of religious experience submitted to the Religious Experience Research Unit at Oxford, 18 percent were visions. See Alister Hardy, *The Spiritual Nature of Man: A Study of Contemporary Religious Experience* (Oxford, England: Clarendon Press, 1979), pp. 26, 32–34, 143.

26. Isa. 6.1–13; Dan. 7.1–14.

27. Jer. 1.11–13; Amos 7.1–3.

28. Goodman's work is extremely interesting and helpful. See *Ecstasy, Ritual, and Alternate Reality* (Bloomington: Indiana University Press, 1988); *Where the Spirits Ride the Wind: Trance Journeys and Other Ecstatic Experiences* (Bloomington: Indiana University Press, 1990), in which she describes extensive experiments involving a variety of postures as a way of entering visionary states. See also her article "Visions," in *Encyclopedia of Religion,* vol. 15, ed. Mircea Elíade and Charles Adams (New York: Macmillan, 1987), pp. 282–88. In much of Western psychiatry, Goodman notes, "seeing things not perceivable to the outside observer is termed *hallucination*" and considered to be

psychotic and a symptom of insanity. But clinically healthy people have visions; moreover, "the religious specialists of uncounted small societies" and "founders of religions such as Buddha, Jesus, or Mohammed were certainly not insane" and "left no doubt that they considered what they saw in trance not an illusion but simply another reality" (*Ecstasy, Ritual, and Alternate Reality*, p. 43).

29. Goodman, "Visions," p. 282 (italics added).

30. For an introduction to shamanism, see articles (with extensive bibliographies) under "Shamanism" in *Encyclopedia of Religion,* vol. 13, by Mircea Elíade, Anna-Leena Siikala, Sam Gill, and Peter Furst, pp. 201–23.

31. These phrases are from Sam Gill's article on North American shamans, *Encyclopedia of Religion,* p. 217.

32. The title of McGinn's projected four-volume study of Christian mysticism also makes the point: *The Presence of God: A History of Western Christian Mysticism.* Volume one is *The Foundations of Mysticism* (New York: Crossroad, 1991); quotation from p. xvii (italics added). See pp. 265–343 for a valuable survey of the modern study of mysticism, including theological, philosophical, comparativist, and psychological approaches. Earlier classical and accessible studies of mysticism include James, *Varieties of Religious Experience,* esp. lectures 16–17; and Evelyn Underhill, *Mysticism: A Study in the Nature and Development of Man's Spiritual Consciousness,* 12th ed. (Cleveland and New York: World, 1965; 1st ed. published in 1911).

33. Quoted by Leech, *Experiencing God,* p. 332.

34. Quoted in McGinn, *Foundations of Mysticism,* p. 273.

35. Reinhold Niebuhr, one of the most influential American Protestant theologians in the middle third of this century, said that mysticism begins with "mist," has "I" in the middle, and ends in "schism" (reported by Smith in *Jesus at 2000,* p. 109). Leech, *Experiencing God,* p. 334, notes that Karl Barth treated mysticism and atheism together (in Barth's *Church Dogmatics* 1.2 [1936], 318ff). See McGinn, *Foundations of Mysticism,* pp. 267–69, for the negative judgments of Albrect Ritschl and Adolf Harnack, influential Protestant theologians from the late nineteenth century.

36. For these two types, see W. T. Stace, *Mysticism and Philosophy* (New York: Macmillan, 1960), who got the distinction from Rudolf Otto, *Mysticism: East and West* (New York: Macmillan, 1970; first published in 1932).

37. Heschel, *Man Is Not Alone: A Philosophy of Religion* (New York: Farrar, Straus & Giroux, 1951), p. 22. For "radical amazement" as a central element in religious experience for Heschel, see pp. 3–79, esp. pp. 11–17, and *God in Search of Man,* pp. 33–87.

38. Because many readers may be familiar with Abraham Maslow's "peak experiences," I note that these experiences probably belong in this category. They involve a radical shift in perception ("B-cognition," Maslow's somewhat inelegant term for "cognition of Being"), a momentary melting away of the ego and ego concerns, and often a transformative effect on the person. Maslow argues that peak experiences are "the core religious experience," even as he affirms that they can be experienced in a completely secular way. See Maslow, *Religions, Values, and Peak-Experiences* (Columbus, OH: Ohio State University Press, 1964).

39. E. F. Edinger, *Ego and Archetype* (Baltimore: Penguin, 1973), pp. 3–4.

40. On the popular level, Raymond Moody's *Life after Life* (New York: Bantam, 1976) is a good introduction. See also Michael Sabom, *Recollections of Death: A Medical Investigation* (New York: Harper & Row, 1982). For recent research, see Arthur S. and Joyce Berger, *Fear of the Unknown* (Westport, CT: Praeger, 1995). A recent anthology is Lee W. Bailey and Jenny Yates, ed., *The Near-Death Experience* (New York: Routledge, 1996). See also Chapter Seven of this book.

41. In a number of workshops, I have asked people whether they have had one or more experiences that they would identify as an experience of God and, if so, to share them in small groups. On average, 80 percent of the participants identify one or more and are eager to talk about them. They also frequently report that they had never before been asked that question in a church setting or given an opportunity to talk about it.

42. Martin Buber, *I and Thou,* trans. by Walter Kaufmann (New York: Scribner's, 1970; originally published in German in 1922 as *Ich und Du*). Except in the title of the book, Kaufmann's translation replaces "I-Thou" with "I-You." German *du* is the familiar and intimate form of "you," and though "thou" in archaic English was the familiar form, in modern English "thou" sounds formal and rev-

erential. (I can recall protests against replacing "thou" in older forms of the English Bible with "you" on the grounds that "you" sounds insufficiently reverential.) Thus Kaufmann argues correctly that "you" is a better translation of *du* than "thou." I have followed his practice.

43. Buber, *I and Thou*, pp. 84–85. Lest the I-It world seem simply negative, it is important to note that we cannot live without it; it is the world of ordered existence. Buber expresses this in a passage that ends with this sobering thought: "And in all the seriousness of truth, listen: without It a human being cannot live. But whoever lives only with that is not human" (p. 85).

44. Buber, *I and Thou*, p. 146.

45. To illustrate with a few examples, many of us have experienced this melting away of ego awareness in moments of falling in love, or becoming absorbed in music, or being overwhelmed by the beauty of nature, or experiencing intense empathy, or (I am told) giving birth. The list is illustrative, not limiting.

46. Maurice Friedman, *Martin Buber's Life and Work,* vol. 3: *The Later Years, 1945–1965* (New York: E. P. Dutton, 1983), p. 381.

47. According to the Religious Experience Research Unit at Oxford (see note 25 in this chapter), the two most common affective elements reported were a sense of "security, protection, and peace" (25 percent) and "joy, happiness, and well-being" (21 percent) (Hardy, *The Spiritual Nature of Man,* pp. 26, 29, 52–53).

48. Quoted by Benjamin Walker, *The Hindu World,* vol. 2 (New York: Praeger, 1968), p. 475.

49. James, *The Varieties of Religious Experience,* pp. 249, 256.

50. Reported by Hardy, *The Spiritual Nature of Man,* p. 53.

51. Abbott, *Flatland* (New York: New American Library, 1984; originally published in 1884).

52. Heschel, *God in Search of Man,* p. 121 (italics in original).

53. In the same passage, Heschel adds, "What we attempt to do in the act of reflection [i.e., thinking about God] is to raise that preconceptual awareness to the level of understanding."

54. Bonhoeffer, *Letters and Papers from Prison,* p. 282.

55. On the question of whether it is appropriate to refer to Augustine as a mystic, see McGinn, *The Foundations of Mysticism,* pp. 228–31. McGinn himself affirms descriptions of Augustine as "the Prince of Mystics" and "the Father of Christian mysticism" (p. 231).

56. Augustine, *Confessions* 10.27, cited by Leech, *Experiencing God,* pp. 324–25 (italics added).

57. McGinn, *Foundations of Mysticism,* p. 240.

58. From an audiotape of Merton made in 1965. I thank Rev. David McConnell, pastor of the United Methodist Church in Lewistown, Montana, for providing me with the quotation.

59. Elizabeth Barrett Browning, *Aurora Leigh,* book 7, lines 821–24, ed. Margaret Reynolds (Athens: Ohio University Press, 1992; originally published in 1857), p. 487.

60. Wordsworth, *Tintern Abbey,* 2.93–108; Andrew J. George, ed., *The Complete Poetical Works of William Wordsworth* (Boston: Houghton Mifflin Co., 1904), p. 92. For a persuasive case that Wordsworth was a panentheist and not a pantheist, see Daniel Dombrowski, "Wordsworth's Panentheism," *Wordsworth Circle 16* (1985): 136–42.

61. Augustine, *Homily on Psalm 99.6,* cited by Leech, *Experiencing God,* p. 324.

62. Buber, *The Prophetic Faith* (New York: Harper & Row, 1949), p. 37; and *On the Bible: Eighteen Studies,* ed. by Nahum Glatzer (New York: Schocken, 1982), pp. 56–57 (excerpt originally published in Buber's *Moses,* 1945). Buber argues that the most satisfactory explanation of the origin of "Yahweh" goes back to the Semitic "Yah, Yahu, or Yahuvah," all of which translate roughly as "He, this one, this is it, oh he!" Buber comments, "This elemental sound was apparently common to the west Semitic tribes, who hinted by it in a mysterious and enthusiastic way to the deity whose name could not be designated."

63. Mitchell, "Sinai," in *Parables and Portraits* (New York: Harper Perennial, 1991), p. 66.

64. To clarify: I am not suggesting that third-person language never be used for God, nor am I suggesting that the solution for the problem of gendered language about God is always to use "You." Rather, the anecdote illustrates the claim that God is present.

65. Buber, *The Way of Response,* ed. N. N. Glatzer (New York: Schocken Books, 1971), pp. 38–39.

PART 2

IMAGING

GOD

CHAPTER 3

IMAGING GOD:

WHY AND
HOW IT
MATTERS

*Tell me your image of God,
and I will tell you your theology.*[1]

Thus far we have been concerned with two root concepts for thinking about God. These root concepts are clothed with a variety of images of God, to which we now turn. Images are a more visual and metaphorical way of seeing and speaking about God: God as king, father, mother, shepherd, lover, rock, wind, light, and so forth. Our focus will be on images of God in the biblical and Christian traditions.

Our images of God matter. Just as how we conceptualize God affects what we think the Christian life is about, so do our images of God. Ideas (which include both concepts and images) are like families: they have relationships. How we image God shapes not only what we think God is like but also what we think the Christian life is about. People who think of God as a warrior may become warriors themselves, whether in a Christian crusade, a Muslim jihad, or an apocalyptically oriented militia. People who think of God as righteous are likely to emphasize righteousness themselves, just as those who think of God as compassionate are likely to emphasize compassion. People who think God is angry at the world are likely to be angry at the world themselves.

In this chapter I will explore what is at stake in how we image God. After some comments about the large variety of metaphors for the sacred in the Bible, I will describe two very different foundational images of God, or models of God, around which these metaphors have commonly been clustered. Each model has crucial consequences for how we image God and the Christian life, including its internal dynamics and its perceptions of nature, society, and gender.

BIBLICAL IMAGES OF GOD: MULTIPLE METAPHORS

We begin with an obvious but important fact: the Bible contains many images of God. Indeed, their multiplicity is striking. They are drawn from a number of areas of human experience:

Political leadership: God as king, lord, warrior, judge, lawgiver

Everyday human life: God as builder, gardener, shepherd, potter, doctor or healer, father, mother, lover, wise woman, old man, woman giving birth, friend

Nature and inanimate objects: God as eagle, lion, bear, hen, fire, light, cloud, wind, breath, rock, fortress, and shield[2]

The large number of biblical images for God has an immediate implication: multiplicity points to metaphoricity. That is, it implies the use of metaphor. Obviously, God cannot literally be all of these. Nor is it the case that God is literally one of these (for example, king or father) and metaphorically the rest. Though theoretically possible, it is not an actual possibility. The reason lies in the ineffability of God: language about God must be metaphorical. Direct nonmetaphorical description of God is impossible. All of these images are metaphors.[3]

The defining characteristic of metaphor is comparison: something is like something else.[4] As such, metaphors are intrinsically nonliteral. A metaphor affirms, even as it also implicitly denies: x is y, x is not y.[5]

Importantly, though metaphors are not literally true, they can nevertheless be true. To use a familiar example, I might say, "My love is a red red rose." Obviously, my love is *not* a red red rose (unless, perhaps, I were a fanatically devoted rose gardener). Rather, there is an implicit "like" in the statement: my love is like a red red rose: beautiful; a source of joy; fragrant; perhaps ephemeral (it blooms for a short time). It would be a wooden-minded literalist who could not understand the metaphor when it is used about one's beloved.

Metaphors are evocative. Suggestive of more than one meaning, they are resonant; they have multiple associations and cannot be translated into a single equivalent literal statement.[6] In the minds of those who created the biblical images of God, there was something about each image that they thought of as like God. To see the evocative power of these metaphors, we need to ask about each in turn, What does "light" (wind, rock, king, lover, mother, father, breath, and so on) as an image for God suggest? What makes each a good image for the sacred?

I provide two examples. First, what does "king" as an image for God suggest? Given the status and role of kings in the ancient world in which the Bible originated, the following might be suggested (some are true of virtually all kings, others only of "ideal" kings):

> *Grandeur, majesty, and glory:* The king's palace, court, and clothing were typically splendid, almost from another world compared to the meager simplicity of peasant existence.
>
> *Power and authority:* The king was the most powerful person and central authority figure in the kingdom.
>
> *Lawgiver and judge:* The king was the source and enforcer of law and thus the source of order in the kingdom. As one who created order out of chaos, the image of king became associated with creation.
>
> *Justice:* Though earthly kings were often in fact unjust, the ideal king would be a champion of justice.
>
> *Protection:* The king protected the kingdom against enemies and became a warrior king if necessary.

And, of course, kings were male.

To cite another example, what is it about "fire" that makes it an image for the sacred? What associations does fire have? Without trying to be comprehensive, I suggest the following:

> *Safety, protection, and warmth:* a campfire at night
>
> *Danger, destruction, fear:* fire and death, including fire and military conquest
>
> *Purifying agent:* as in the process of refining
>
> *Light:* fire is a source of light, safety, and protection in the night; it can also be a beacon.

Moreover, fire is *mysterious and ethereal.* Most of us can recall staring at a log fire as it burns low, the flames moving slowly around the logs, flickering, disappearing, reappearing; suddenly we wonder: *What is it?* The flames seem ethereal, almost nonmaterial, yet they are manifestly real. To the ancient mind (as it does sometimes to us), fire appeared to be a mysterious nonmaterial reality that was simultaneously life-giving, powerful, dangerous, purifying, and enlightening.

I need not multiply the examples to make the point: biblical metaphors for God are evocative, carrying many rich associations. Of course, one needs to be thoughtful about which of a metaphor's associations might be transferred to God. For instance, one can cook on a fire, but it seems metaphorically irrelevant.

Importantly, many of these metaphors are relational, imaging not only God but ourselves in relationship to God. To be elementary, in relation to God as shepherd, we are sheep; in relation to God as parent, we are children; in relation to God as king, we are subjects; in relation to God as lover, we are the beloved. Sometimes the relationship is complex and ambiguous: in relationship to God as warrior, we might be either "soldiers of the Lord" engaged in a holy war, or the enemy, or passive benefactors as God wars on our behalf.

CATEGORIES OF BIBLICAL IMAGES

The diversity of biblical images of God can also be appreciated by sorting them into categories. *Anthropomorphic* images portray God in humanlike form: God as king, lord, judge, lawgiver, potter, shepherd, wise woman, father, mother, lover, healer, and so forth. *Nonanthropomorphic* (nonhumanlike) images speak of God as rock, fire, light, eagle, lion, bear, hen, cloud, wind, breath, fortress, shield.

A second category consists of *images of distance* and *images of closeness.* Images of distance include especially "king" and the metaphors associated with king: lawgiver, judge, warrior, and so forth. The king was distant: he did not live among the people but in a walled city or palace, most often on a high place. Ordinary people did not often or ever associate with the king; peasants were not invited to royal banquets. So also with "father": in the framework of the patriarchal family, the father was most often a distant figure, a little king within his family. Often the father (and other men of the family) lived in quarters separate from women and children. Images of closeness, on the other hand, include shepherd, mother, lover, friend, healer, shield, fortress, and breath.

A third category comprises *male and female images*. Male images are by far more common. This is not surprising, given that the Bible originated in a patriarchal culture and in competition with religious traditions that had both male and female deities. What is more surprising is that female images are sometimes used: God as nurturing mother, woman giving birth, wise woman, and mother bird. There are other images that can apply equally well to either sex: shepherd (both women and men were shepherds), potter, lover, friend. Moreover, the Hebrew word *ruach* (which means spirit, breath, and wind) is feminine in gender.[7] Thus there is biblical warrant for female images of God.

CLUSTERING THE IMAGES: TWO MODELS OF GOD

In the biblical and Christian traditions, these metaphors have commonly clustered around two primary "models" of God. A model is a gestalt— that is, a foundational or root image. As a gestalt or foundational image, each model constellates several metaphors into a coherent pattern that also images God's relationship to us and to the world.[8] Each model of God thus goes with a model of the Christian life.

The first model, which I will call "the monarchical model,"[9] clusters together images of God as king, lord, and father; it leads to a "performance model" of the Christian life. The second model clusters together images of God that point to intimate relationship and belonging. I will call it "the Spirit model"; it leads to a "relational model" of the Christian life.[10]

Both models and visions of the Christian life are found throughout all periods of Christian history, though the first is more common. From roughly the fourth century—when Christianity became the dominant religion of Western culture—through the present, the monarchical model has dominated. But alongside it, as an alternative voice, the Spirit model has also persisted. Though features from each model are commonly combined into a synthesis, usually by incorporating the second into the first, it is illuminating to see them as contrasting models of God and contrasting visions of the Christian life. They reflect two different voices within the Christian tradition.

THE MONARCHICAL MODEL OF
GOD AND THE CHRISTIAN LIFE

The central elements of this model are found in the root image of God as a king. Put most compactly, God is imaged as a male authority figure who is the ruler of the universe. As with an earthly king, images of domination and subjection are central to this model. The model has profound consequences for our images of ourselves, the internal dynamics of the religious life, and the world.

Because I will be quite critical of this model, I want to begin by emphasizing that the biblical use of the image of God as king does not have just one meaning and does not intrinsically generate the monarchical model. In the Bible, the image of God as king has two very different—indeed, opposing—meanings. On the one hand, God as king is spoken of as the origin, legitimator, and enforcer of the social order. Not only is God the lawgiver from whom the society's structures of order come (its laws, practices, and institutions), as well as the judge who enforces them, God is also the legitimator of the king's position at the top of a hierarchical social order centered in Jerusalem. God's dwelling place on earth was in Jerusalem, which was also the home of the king. According to the royal theology of the Hebrew Bible, the king in Jerusalem was no less than the son of God, and God had promised to him and his descendants perpetual rule.[11] The social order (with its religious, political, and economic components) was ordained and guaranteed by God.

On the other hand, the image of God as king is used in a very different way: not to legitimate but to subvert existing social structures. In the voices of Moses, the prophets, Jesus, and much of the New Testament, God as king not only relativizes every earthly kingship but often becomes the basis for radical criticism of and opposition to the existing social order. The conflict between the lordship of God and the lordship of pharaoh, the kingship of God and the kings of Israel and Judah, the kingship of Herod and the kingship of Jesus, and the lordship of Christ and the lordship of Caesar, sounds throughout the tradition. It is a truly subversive voice, with a very different vision of individual and social existence for humankind.

But what I am focusing on now is the way the image of God as king functions *within the common form of the monarchical model*. The model has its own logic.

The Monarchical Model

Because an earthly king is male, God is imaged as *male*. The image of God as king is not only anthropomorphic but andromorphic (*andros* is the Greek word for male). Hence I will use the masculine pronoun in this section. Like an earthly king, God is powerful, but he is even more than that: God is *all-powerful*—that is, omnipotent. Like an earthly king, God is the *lawgiver and judge,* but with even more serious consequences. Our well-being in this world—and, in later layers of the biblical tradition, our eternal destiny as well—depend on our observance of his law.[12] Finally, the image of God as king suggests that God is *distant*. The distance between an earthly king—politically, economically, and architecturally, as well as in power, wealth, and lifestyle—and peasants, the ordinary people of the time, was immense.

In relationship to this image of God, who are we? What image of ourselves goes with God as king? We are subjects and therefore "not much." In relation to God as king, we are peasants. Moreover, as subjects, what we owe to the king is loyalty and obedience. But we are not very good at this. Here the image of the king as lawgiver and judge makes its impact. Legal metaphors and legal logic are pervasive in the monarchical model. We are disobedient and disloyal subjects (with disloyalty usually defined as disobedience). Sin is any violation of God's law, the religious equivalent of a violation of the earthly king's law, and just as crime deserves punishment, so does sin. Within this model, we have offended against divine majesty, and we deserve judgment.

But God as king also loves his subjects (this model knows about, and can incorporate, the love of God). This creates a dilemma, and the legal logic continues to unfold. As lawgiver and judge, the king has laws that must be enforced; as one who also loves his people, he desires to be merciful (itself a legal term).[13] And so the king creates a way for his people to compensate for their sins and escape the punishment they deserve. Namely, sacrifices can be offered to God to atone for disobedience. What is required are compensation and contrition, appropriate sacrifice and true repentance. In the royal theology of ancient Israel, this was institutionalized in the temple in Jerusalem.

In the Christian version of the monarchical model, the king's love is seen especially in Jesus. Jesus is the only beloved son of God the king. Because God loves us, he sends his son into the world to die on the cross for us and for our salvation, as the sacrifice required by God the lawgiver and judge; this sacrifice makes our forgiveness possible. Moreover, because Jesus is God's only son and has been sent by God, the sacrifice is ultimately made by God. So deep is God's love for us that God provides the sacrifice.

In this fashion the Christian form of the monarchical model resolves the tension between God's love and God as lawgiver and judge. It is by being Christians that we are able to take part in the benefits conferred by Jesus' death. Through some combination of believing in Jesus, true repentance, and good works, we are reconciled with God as king, lawgiver, and judge.

Finally, it is important to note how the image of God as king assimilates other images of God. "Lord" is a virtual synonym. "Father" (though it can have other meanings) within the context of the patriarchal family functions in the same way: a somewhat distant male authority figure to whom obedience is owed. God as creator is frequently described using royal imagery: like a king ordering his kingdom, God the creator brings order out of chaos. The humble image of "shepherd" is sometimes assimilated: because David, the greatest of Israel's kings, was a shepherd, the ideal king is the shepherd king. God as shepherd becomes God as king. Within this model, even Jesus, whose message and activity profoundly subverted the imagery and ideology of kingship, becomes the king who will judge at the last judgment.

The Effects of the Model

Popular Christianity has been very much shaped by "the myth of the crown" enshrined within the monarchical model.[14] As Sallie McFague notes, this model is "so prevalent in mainstream Christianity that it is often not recognized as a picture" but instead "accepted as the natural understanding of the relationship of God and the world."[15] Because of this model's prevalence, it is important to analyze its effects.

EFFECTS ON THE IMAGE OF GOD

God as a Distant Powerful Being. As already noted, the monarchical model with its root image of God as king suggests distance. It is a distance of both power and place. Like a king ruling over his kingdom, God's power and authority stand over the world. Like a king living in his walled palace high on a hill, God is separate from the world. Thus the image of God as distant king and lord goes with the concept of God that I described in Chapter One, the all-powerful god of supernatural theism. Indeed, the monarchical model of God provided the clothing for my childhood concept of God as a supernatural being. Though I imaged God more as a father than as a king, it amounted to the same thing: God as a powerful male authority figure "out there." The monarchical image of God thus has the same problems as does the concept of God as a supernatural being separate from the world.

God as Male. The monarchical model uses male images to speak of God. This has consequences not only for the lives of women but also for the lives of men, a point to which I will soon return.

God as Lawgiver and Judge. As noted, this model can speak powerfully of the love of God. But it does so within the legal framework and logic of the model itself: God as lawgiver and judge; sin as violation of God's laws; people as guilty and deserving of punishment; compensation as necessary; God as merciful and therefore offering another way of becoming righteous (namely, through Jesus); and at the end, a final judgment with eternal rewards and punishments.

Thus, even when the model incorporates Jesus as the sacrifice offered for us, it essentially leaves intact the image of God as lawgiver and judge and images the Christian life within the framework of law.[16]

EFFECTS: A "PERFORMANCE MODEL"
OF THE CHRISTIAN LIFE

The monarchical model's use of legal metaphors and legal logic to image the relationship between humans and the divine shapes the internal dynamics of the Christian life into a performance model. It does so in three closely related ways. First, the model makes sin and guilt central. Sin (understood as disobedience to God) is the most important problem. The model's emphasis on sin affects other key Christian notions, whose rich resonances of meaning are thereby impoverished and even distorted. Repentance becomes contrition for sin, redemption becomes redemption from sin, liberation becomes liberation from sin, and salvation becomes salvation from sin. The model in effect co-opts the tradition by becoming a comprehensive lens through which the tradition is seen.

Roberta Bondi's recollection of the centrality of sin in her childhood Christianity makes the point well:

> Sin was what religion was about. If you had asked me in the fourth grade, "Why was Jesus born?" I would have been glad to answer, "It was because of sin. Jesus was born in order to pay the price for our sin by suffering and dying on the cross." If you had pushed me about what it took to get our sins forgiven, I would have told you: "We have to repent of our sins." If you had pushed me a little further to ask, "And what does it mean to repent?" I would have said, "To feel really, really bad about what a sinful person you are."[17]

The emphasis on sin thus affects not only the way the whole Christian story is told but also confers an identity. It leads to the internal dynamic of thinking of oneself primarily as a sinner who needs to repent, and it defines repentance as feeling really bad about oneself. To be sure, we may also be forgiven sinners, but the definitive characterization of us as sinful and guilty remains.

Second, this model easily confuses God with the superego and the Christian life with life under the superego. The superego is the critical voice in our psyches, a voice that stands over us in judgment, offering praise or blame.[18] The superego is the storehouse of *oughts* and *shoulds* within us, the cumulative product of messages received in our socialization about what we should do and how we ought to live. Most often, it is experienced as a punitive voice. Life under the superego is a life of continually trying to measure up; it is life under the law. Yet life under the superego is the most common adult way of being, the natural product of our socialization.

The monarchical model of God commonly reinforces the superego. The internal dynamics of the model and the superego are the same: the superego functions in our minds as a little king, an internal lawgiver and judge. It is thus easy to confuse the voice of the superego with the voice of God, especially when the voice of the superego has Christian content. God becomes "the internalized overseer, the policeman who never sleeps."[19] More lightheartedly, it is God imaged as a high school principal unhappily leafing through our records.[20] When this happens, the Christian life becomes confused with life under the punitive superego. We are never good enough.

Life under the superego exists in secular forms as well, of course. Indeed, one can make a good case that it is a nearly universal human condition, a central dimension of the human predicament from which we need deliverance.[21] Moreover, it seems to me that the great and formative voices of the biblical and Christian tradition address this need: they speak of liberation from life under the punitive superego.[22] Thus it is more than ironic that the monarchical model of Christianity reinforces the superego.[23]

Third, within the monarchical model of God, the internal dynamic of the Christian life becomes "meeting requirements" or "measuring up." The image of God as lawgiver and judge (even when qualified by the notion that God, through Jesus, provides the sacrifice for sin) makes it clear that God has requirements that must be met, either by obeying God's laws or by performing alternative service (typically involving belief in Jesus, sincere repentance, and perhaps penance). But either way, the *system* of requirements remains; only the *content* of what is required is changed. The monarchical model thereby suggests that the Christian life is about meeting God's requirements (whether few or many), even though it may also entail more than that.[24]

Thus the monarchical model of God generates a "performance model" of the Christian life. Our eternal destiny depends on how well we "perform," on whether we believe or do what is necessary in order to be saved. The self is perpetually "on trial." This understanding of God and our relationship to God, of course, leaves us with the finger-shaking God of my childhood.

People struggle with the internal dynamics generated by this model. It is not a comfortable model. It generates guilt. It may also reinforce guilt that is already present for other reasons. Historically, some Christians have broken through it to an experience of a God of grace behind it. Indeed, for some, intensification of law and guilt to the breaking point has been the means of breaking through. This has been a classic pattern, and because of Martin Luther's own religious experience, it is the classic Lutheran and more broadly Protestant approach. But the intensification of guilt is a dangerous tiger to ride. It can easily leave one simply feeling sinful and guilty with no release, no breakthrough into a world of grace.

People struggle with this model for yet another reason. Many in the modern world (including many Christians) find this model and the way it shapes the Christian story increasingly unbelievable. Perhaps our ancestors several generations back could believe it with less difficulty. But for us, the awareness of global religious pluralism and of the cultural origins of religion and its social and psychological functions makes it difficult to believe that the Christian story as gestalted by the monarchical model is true in any literal sense of the word. Thus its final contribution to the internal dynamics of the Christian life is that it makes it seem incredible.

EFFECTS: CHRISTIAN PERCEPTIONS OF NATURE, SOCIETY, AND GENDER

The monarchical model shapes not only the internal dynamics of the Christian life but also Christian perceptions of nature, politics, and gender. Its central image of domination and subjection goes with the domination of nature by humans, the domination of other human beings by political and economic elites, and the domination of women by men. It is not the singular cause of any of these, but it is part of the ideological package that has legitimated domination.

Nature. Three effects seem most important. First, the monarchical model's image of God as distant from the world means that God is separate from nature. Within this framework, creation is seen as a product, as something God produces separate from Godself; God is related to nature as a potter is to a pot. Though God might choose to *appear* in nature or natural phenomena, God is not *in* nature nor is nature in God. The radical separation of the world from the sacred means that nature is nothing special. It is not holy or sacred in any sense of the word.[25] Moreover, this model's image of God as lawgiver and judge relates God exclusively to human beings and leaves God unrelated to the nonhuman world.[26]

Second, this model leads to a "domination over" understanding of the relationship between human beings and nature. Just as God has dominion over the universe, so human beings created in the image of God have been given dominion over nature.[27] We are little kings in our relationship with nature.

Third, this reinforces an anthropocentric view of nature, one that sees nature in terms of its value for humans. Nature has been given to humankind; it is there for us and our use.[28] Nature has instrumental value, not intrinsic value.

Though it is simplistic to say that the attitude toward nature as enshrined in the monarchical model is the primary cause of the contemporary environmental crisis, many analysts persuasively claim that it has played a major ideological role.[29] It has contributed to the mind-set of modern anthropocentric views of nature.[30]

Society. A monarchical model of God and a monarchical political order go together. To state the obvious, the metaphor of God as king originated in such societies. But more is meant. Namely, the monarchical model of God has most often functioned to legitimate what Walter Wink calls "the domination system," the most common form of political society over the course of recorded history.[31] Domination systems are hierarchical social orders marked by economic exploitation and political oppression in which a few people (almost always men) rule over everybody else.

Though the image of God as king can be used to challenge domination systems (as noted earlier), more commonly it legitimates the earthly king's rule and the social order over which he presides. God as king is the source of the society's values, laws, and structure, and the king rules as the vice-regent of God. Microcosm mirrors macrocosm; the earthly king's rule replicates the rule of the divine sovereign. The king is the number one figure in the domination system, and his role at its pinnacle reflects the will of God. Chosen by God or anointed by God, the king rules by divine decree, a status frequently ritualized by the participation of religious officials in the king's coronation. The result is a domination system legitimated by God.

Gender. Once again, the image of God and the structure of society go together. Historically, male images of God go with a male-dominated society (including male political figures, religious figures, and heads of family). The result is patriarchy, defined as a hierarchical social structure dominated by men. Patriarchal politics, patriarchal religion, and the patriarchal family are all connected to the monarchical model of God. God as a male monarch legitimates the domination of men over women. As Mary Daly put it over two decades ago, when God is male, the male is God.[32]

Gender differences are also attached to this model's dualistic separation between God and the world of nature. For much of Western history, God has been personified as male and nature as female. We still speak of Mother Earth. We also speak of the conquest of nature and the rape of nature. Moreover, women are associated with matter, body, and feeling, while men are associated with spirit, mind, and reason. Women are closer to the earth, men closer to God. And just as nature is to be subdued by humans, the body by the mind, emotions by reason, so women are to be subordinate to men.

Feminist theology has highlighted the dominance of male images of God in the Christian tradition and the social and psychological consequences of imaging God as a male authority figure. Obviously, the question of the gender of God language is a crucial issue for women.[33] Not only has patriarchy been politically and socially oppressive of women, depriving them of full participation in the life of both church and culture, but imaging God as male impacts women's identity as well. How can women be in the image of God if God cannot be imaged in female form? Thus something is at stake for women in particular.

But this is not of importance simply for women. Rather, the emergence of feminist theology seems to me to be the single most important development in theology in my lifetime.[34] Not only has it made us aware of the pervasive effects of the monarchical model but it has provided another vantage point—another lens—for seeing the tradition as a whole. It is thus of great significance for both women and men, for the monarchical model profoundly affects men's lives, too. Though the model has given a place of great privilege to some men (the elites at the top of patriarchal systems) and a place of some privilege to most men (in the family, church, and many occupations), it has also legitimated political structures oppressive of both men and women. And, obviously, the negative effects of the model's perception of nature affect us all.

In yet one more way male gender images for God affect both men and women. Namely, the internal dynamic of the Christian life as measuring up to God the lawgiver and judge is intensified by male imagery for the sacred. I share two anecdotes to illustrate the point. The first is a story told by a woman pastor about a confirmation class she taught.[35] While teaching a unit on prayer, she asked her class of eighth graders to write answers to a number of questions. One question was "When you pray, what do you call God?" For all of them, their number one answer was "Father." Another question was "When you pray, what do you pray for?" Number one on all of their lists was "forgiveness." Is that a coincidence? If they had routinely prayed to God as mother rather than father, would they still have made forgiveness their number one prayer request, their most urgent need?

The second anecdote comes from watching my wife in her role as an Episcopal priest distributing the bread of the Eucharist one Sunday morning. Among the people kneeling at the altar rail was a four-year-old girl, looking up expectantly at my wife's face as she bent down to give her a piece of bread. My wife has a beautiful face and a wonderful smile. As I watched the little girl, I suddenly wondered if my wife's face was filling her visual screen and being imprinted in her mind as an image of God, much as the face of the male pastor from my childhood had been imprinted in mine. And I was struck by the difference: an image of God as a male authority figure shaking his finger at us versus an image of God as a beautiful loving woman bending down to feed us. Of course, I do not know what was happening in that little girl's mind, but the difference in images is dramatic. In that difference, something is at stake for both men and women.

Because I have been quite critical of the monarchical model of God and its consequences, I want to emphasize as I end this section that this model has, almost in spite of itself, nourished the lives of millions of Christians through the centuries. The images of God as king, lord, and father have been an important part of Christian devotion. Moreover, for many Christians who use the monarchical model to think of God, the love of God is nevertheless central (and indeed triumphs over the model). What I have been talking about is what happens within the logic of the monarchical model itself. We turn now to a different model for imaging God and God's relationship to the world.

A DIFFERENT MODEL: GOD AS SPIRIT

How to name this model is not so obvious. The phrase "monarchical model" flows naturally out of its root metaphor of God as king. But no single metaphor so clearly epitomizes the alternative model. In the absence of an obvious choice, I suggest "Spirit" as a root image for this model of God, and the phrase "Spirit model" as a designator for the model itself. It leads to an image of the Christian life that stresses relationship, intimacy, and belonging.

The Spirit Model

As a root metaphor for the sacred, Spirit images God as a nonmaterial reality pervading the universe as well as being more than the universe. As used in the Bible (and as used here), its meaning is broader than the specific Christian doctrine of "the Holy Spirit," which sees it as one aspect of God. But in the Bible, Spirit is used comprehensively to refer to God's presence in creation, in the history of Israel, and in the life of Jesus and the early church. Its meaning is sufficiently broad to make it a synonym for the sacred. Spirit "evokes a universal perspective and signifies divine activity in its widest reaches."[36] Strongly associated with God's presence in and engagement with the world (God's immanence), Spirit also points to God's transcendence. It images "God's ongoing transcending engagement with the world."[37]

Some of its resonances of meaning are suggested by the Hebrew word for Spirit. *Ruach* also means wind and breath. The associations of both are suggestive. Both are invisible yet manifestly real. We cannot see the wind, though its presence and effects are felt; it moves without being seen. When it blows, it is all around us. Breath is like wind inside the body. For the ancient Hebrews (as for us), it was associated with life. Metaphorically, God as Spirit is both wind and breath, a nonmaterial reality outside of us and within us. Our breath is God breathing us, and God is as near to us as our own breath. Speaking of God as Spirit, as both wind and breath, evokes both transcendence and nearness.[38]

The monarchical model also affirms that God is Spirit, of course. The king who rules the universe is not a flesh-and-blood king. But there is a difference: when Spirit is assimilated to the monarchical model, God is not Spirit but *a* spirit—that is, a spiritual being who is out there, not here. But when Spirit is not domesticated and diminished by the monarchical model, Spirit retains the suggestive meanings associated with breath and wind: God is the encompassing Spirit both within us and outside us.

Specific Metaphors for God as Spirit

The model of God as Spirit is clothed with a number of more specific metaphors. As we shall see, their associations are different in important ways from God as king, lord, and father.

Nonanthropomorphic Metaphors.   There are a number of nonanthropomorphic images in addition to wind and breath. God as "rock" can connote either God's distance or God's closeness.[39] The Hebrew word for rock does not mean a big stone but "cliff"—hence a mountain or high place. God as rock can point to distance: God is in the heights, known at the top of a mountain (as in the Sinai story). God as rock can also evoke closeness. A mountain or high place is a place of refuge and safety; fortresses are built on high places, and a mountain may have caves in which one can hide or seek shelter. Here God as "rock" is something that one can be "on" or "in"; it is a metaphor of nearness.[40] So also fire and light are images of nearness: one must be close enough to a light to see it, close enough to a fire to be warmed (or protected or purified) by it.

God as Mother. Sometimes God as Spirit is imaged as a human mother, sometimes as a mother animal. Resonances include birthing and nurturing.[41] Like a hovering or brooding bird, God as Spirit creates the world. Spirit is like a woman in labor, giving birth. Spirit is like a mother caring for her children and comforting them.[42] One of God's central qualities is compassion, a word that in Hebrew is related to the word for "womb." Not only is compassion a female image suggesting source of life and nourishment but it also has a feeling dimension: God as compassionate Spirit feels for us as a mother feels for the children of her womb.[43] Spirit feels the suffering of the world and participates in it.

God as Intimate Father. In common Christian usage, as previously noted, God as father is most frequently assimilated to the monarchical image of God. But this is quite different from the biblical use of the metaphor. In both the Hebrew Bible and the New Testament, God as father is often used in contexts of intimacy—in contrast to the postbiblical patriarchal use of father within the framework of the monarchical model.[44] Its frequency in the New Testament is probably because of Jesus' use of *abba,* an intimate form of "father."[45] It names God as the intimate father who is close at hand and who may be trusted to give good gifts to his children.[46]

God as Wisdom (Sophia). Another female image for the sacred in the Bible is "the wisdom woman," "the wise woman," or "Sophia."[47] Sophia is the wisdom of God personified as a woman. She is an important figure in Proverbs and in two other works of pre-Christian Jewish wisdom, the Wisdom of Solomon and Ecclesiasticus (sometimes known as

Sirach). The latter two were part of the Christian Bible until the Protestant Reformation of the sixteenth century "demoted" them to "the apocrypha," which gave them a secondary (though still important) status. Though they remain in Catholic and Orthodox Bibles, they are not in many Protestant Bibles, which may help to explain the surprise (and shock) that Sophia language causes in some Protestant circles.[48]

The relationship between Sophia and God is complex. Sometimes Sophia is spoken of as a figure separate from God yet in very close relationship to God.[49] She performs divine functions and thus is the functional equivalent of God. Moreover, there are texts in which the word *Sophia* is used when we would expect the word *God* to be used; the author treats them as interchangeable terms.[50] Thus Sophia is not simply a personification of God's wisdom but also an image or metaphor for God.

Sophia as a metaphor for Spirit is associated especially with Spirit's presence in the world. God as the wise woman is not only the architect and means of creation but is also present in the created order. She is the *Shekinah,* the divine presence dwelling with the Israelites in their history. She speaks through prophets, summons people to live by her wisdom, and invites people to her banquet of bread and wine. Sophia as a metaphor for Spirit suggests closeness and presence, guidance and nourishment.

God as Lover.   Images of God as lover or spouse and of us as God's beloved are found in both the Hebrew Bible and the New Testament. Sometimes marriage imagery is used, and sometimes the language is explicitly sexual. Hosea uses the image of God as lover with particular frequency and power. The Israel of his day is portrayed as the unfaithful beloved who has adulterously strayed from God; like a jealous lover, God is angered, yet yearns for the return of the beloved, alluring her and speaking tenderly to her.[51] In the Song of Songs, whatever its original setting and meaning, the lover-beloved imagery with all of its eroticism has commonly been understood in both Jewish and Christian traditions as a story of the mystical relationship between God the lover and us the beloved.[52] In the New Testament, the church is spoken of as the bride of Christ, who is the bridegroom.

Because the biblical image of God as lover developed within an androcentric and patriarchal culture, the male is typically imaged as the lover and the female as the beloved.[53] But there is nothing intrinsically male about the lover image. It is an anthropomorphic image for Spirit that can be either male or female. The image is particularly rich. Lover and beloved delight in each other. They prize and value each other. They yearn for each other. It can also involve betrayal and jealousy. It is a relationship of extraordinary intimacy. It is a striking image for the divine-human relationship.[54]

God as Journey Companion. Rather than a single image, this is a category of images pointing to God as a companion who travels with us. It includes the pillar of fire by night and the cloud by day that led the Israelites through the wilderness, as well as the presence of God that tented among them in a mobile home (the tabernacle). God as shepherd is another such image, but with the added dimension of nourishment and protection.[55] The shepherd not only travels with the sheep but leads them to water and food, finds shelter, protects them, and seeks them when they go astray.[56] In the New Testament, journey companion imagery is associated especially with Jesus. A disciple is one who journeys with Jesus (who also provides bread for the journey; indeed, "companion" literally means somebody with whom one breaks bread). In the Emmaus Road story, the risen Christ journeys with his disciples, even though they do not recognize him. And in John's gospel, the image of God as shepherd is applied to Jesus: the Johannine Jesus is "the good shepherd."

The Difference This Model Makes

This model leads to a quite different understanding of the Christian life. Though for many of us it points to the God we never knew, it is also a very ancient model of God and vision of the Christian tradition. It springs from an alternative voice (indeed, a chorus of voices) within the biblical tradition, one that counters the monarchical model's version of God and of our relationship to God.

DIFFERENCES: EFFECTS ON THE IMAGE OF GOD

The biblical metaphors for the Spirit model affect our root image of God in three quite obvious ways. First, these metaphors emphasize the nearness of God rather than the distance implied by the monarchical model. They evoke closeness, relationship, and connection. God as

Spirit is near, at hand; indeed, we live within Spirit. Nearness also involves concern: God as Spirit is compassionate. God is the womblike one who gave birth to us, who nurtures us, cares for us, yearns for us. Yet though these metaphors emphasize nearness and immanence, they also affirm transcendence: God as Spirit is more than any of these metaphors, just as Spirit is more than the space-time world.

Second, both male and female metaphors (as well as some that are neither) are used, rather than the exclusively male images of the monarchical model. God is like a woman giving birth, like a mother raising her children, like Sophia the wisdom woman; God is like an intimate father. Moreover, some images go equally well with either gender: God as lover, as companion or friend, even as shepherd. The use of both male and female metaphors makes it clear, of course, that God is neither male nor female, something that we presumably have always known (though the insistence in some circles on male imagery and pronouns makes one wonder).

The awareness that there are female metaphors for God in the Bible is helpful in a time of sensitivity to the impact of gender language: there is biblical warrant for female images. Moreover, this is not simply a matter of linguistic gender equality (important as that is), for these images affect the psyches of both men and women and shape attitudes toward society and nature.

Third, rather than the essentially anthropomorphic image of God as king, lord, and patriarchal father, the metaphors for God as Spirit include both nonanthropomorphic and anthropomorphic images. The presence of both is suggestive. Anthropomorphic images of the sacred are sometimes simply viewed as human projections (which, of course, they are, just as all images of God are). But they are also the natural language of relationship. That is, they suggest that there is a personal dimension to the relationship to God. Yet nonanthropomorphic images suggest that God is not simply a person. Combining the two suggests that the relationship to God is personal, even as God is more than a person. The sacred is not simply a nonanimate mystery but a presence.

To use an ancient image from the Bible, these metaphors lead to a covenantal model of the divine-human relationship. The term *covenant* emphasizes relationship and belonging. It is an intrinsically dialogical model, an "I-You" model of our relationship to the one to whom we belong.

These metaphors also have an affective dimension. They do not simply lead to a set of intellectual conclusions about God's nearness and concern but also affect the feeling level of the psyche. Image God as lover, or as wind and breath, or as nurturing mother, or as "the You" who is present whether we know it or not, or as any of the other images we have reviewed. How does this feel as an image of God, compared to imaging God as a distant king, lawgiver, and judge? How does it feel as an image of yourself in relation to God?

DIFFERENCES: EFFECTS ON KEY CHRISTIAN NOTIONS

The Spirit model of God affects the meaning of a number of central Christian teachings. It does so by changing the framework in which they are seen. Because much of the rest of this book concerns its effects on our vision of the Christian life, I will provide only a couple of illustrative examples here.

Creation looks different. Within the popular version of the monarchical model, God's creation of the world is typically understood as an event in the distant past and as involving the creation of a universe separate from God. The Spirit model, with its emphasis on connectedness, can see God's creation as an ongoing activity: in every moment of time, God as Spirit (as the nonmaterial "ground" of all that is) is bringing the universe into existence. Creation is not about what happened "in the beginning" but about what is always happening. To speak of God as creator is to speak of the ongoing dependence of the universe on Spirit. Spirit is constantly vibrating (to use another metaphor) the world into existence.

The human condition looks different. Our central problem is not sin and guilt, as it is within the monarchical model. For the Spirit model, our central problem is "estrangement," whose specific meaning of "separated from that to which one belongs" is most appropriate.[57] For the Spirit model, we are in God, whether we know it or not; we belong to God, whether we know it or not; and God is present to us, whether we experience that presence or not. But we commonly live our lives "east of Eden," outside of paradise (where paradise is understood to be the manifest presence of God). Our problem is our estrangement, our blindness to the presence of God, our separation from the Spirit who is all around us and within us and to which we belong.

Sin looks different. For the monarchical model, sin is primarily disloyalty to the king, seen especially as disobedience to his laws. The metaphors used to express the Spirit model suggest something else. For the metaphor of God as lover, sin is unfaithfulness—that is, sin is going after other lovers. This is a classic image for idolatry: making something other than Spirit central, giving one's primary loyalty to something other than God. Idolatry—infidelity to God—is the root sin from which more specific acts follow. For the metaphor of God as the compassionate one who cares for all of her children, sin is failure in compassion, whether individually or socially in the form of an unjust society. Sin includes inflicting suffering on those who are also God's creation, as well as being indifferent to their suffering.

Thus sin remains. Only now the emphasis is not on sin as a violation of God's laws but on sin as betrayal of relationship and absence of compassion. Repentance also remains, only now it does not mean primarily sincere contrition for sins committed but a turning and returning to that to which we belong, God as Spirit. Judgment also remains, only now it is not primarily the threat of eternal judgment. Rather, how we live our lives has consequences. Blindness has its effects, both for the individual and the social order. If we remain estranged from God, we will remain unsatisfied and unfulfilled, even desperate. We may experience a "sickness unto death"—that desperate state of needing to die but being unable to do so that is also a state of refusing to be born.[58] The meaning of salvation also changes: it is not primarily in the future and after death, as the monarchical model images it, but is something that happens in the present in our relationship with God as Spirit.[59]

Finally, God as king and lord looks different. When freed from the monarchical model, these images have very different meanings. Both point to the surpassing otherness of God. God as Spirit is glorious, radiant, and splendid, like the splendor of a king. As the source of both life and death, God as Spirit is lord of life and death. Moreover, apart from the monarchical model, these images have a subversive and liberating meaning. Rather than being the legitimator of domination systems, God as king and lord is the subverter of systems of domination. God is lord, not pharaoh; God is king, not the king in Jerusalem; Jesus is king, not the Herods or Caesars of this world; God is lord, not the superego. God as king is the compassionate warrior who grieves with and takes the side of those who suffer under domination systems. Within the model of God as Spirit, monarchical imagery subverts the monarchical model itself.

DIFFERENCES: EFFECTS ON
IMAGING THE CHRISTIAN LIFE

The images of God associated with the Spirit model are rich, and they dramatically affect how we think of the Christian life. Rather than God being a distant being with whom we might spend eternity, Spirit —the sacred—is right here. Rather than God being the lawgiver and judge whose requirements must be met and whose justice must be satisfied, God is the lover who yearns to be in relationship to us. Rather than sin and guilt being the central dynamic of the Christian life, the central dynamic becomes relationship—with God, the world, and each other. The Christian life is about turning toward and entering into relationship with the one who is already in relationship with us—with the one who gave us life, who has loved us from the beginning, and who loves us whether we know that or not, who journeys with us whether we know that or not.

The Christian life thus has at its center becoming conscious of that relationship.[60] It is the response to the words of an unknown prophet who spoke of God's presence and love in Israel's time in exile, the gospel as found in the second half of the book of Isaiah:

> Thus says the Lord, the one who created you, who formed you:
> "Do not be afraid, for I have delivered you. I have called you by name, and you are mine.
> When you pass through the waters, I will be with you; and through the rivers, they shall not overcome you.
> When you walk through fire, you shall not be burned, and the flame shall not consume you.
> You are precious in my sight, and I love you.
> Do not be afraid—for I am with you."[61]

Notes

1. A remark made by a character in a novel I imagine writing.
2. Two recent accessible treatments of biblical images of God are Johanna W. H. van Wijk-Bos, *Reimagining God: The Case for Scriptural Diversity* (Louisville, KY: Westminster John Knox, 1995) and Gail Ramshaw, *God Beyond Gender: Feminist Christian God-Language* (Minneapolis: Fortress, 1995). Wijk-Bos includes illuminating studies of a number of biblical texts; Ramshaw focuses on the use of biblical and Christian images of God in worship and liturgy. Though both books treat feminist issues, their application is much broader.

3. For a fine introduction to metaphor and its role in theology, see Sallie McFague, *Models of God* (Philadelphia: Fortress, 1987), esp. pp. 22–23, 29–40. See also Wijk-Bos, *Reimagining God*, pp. 35–36, and Ian Barbour, *Myths, Models, and Paradigms* (New York: Harper & Row, 1974), pp. 12–16.

4. The Greek roots of metaphor mean "to transfer," "to carry with." A metaphor thus carries meaning or transfers meaning from itself to its referent.

5. McFague, *Models of God*, p. 33: "Metaphor always has the character of 'is' and 'is not.' " See also Paul Ricoeur, "Biblical Hermeneutics," *Semeia 4*, ed. John Dominic Crossan (1975): 88—for metaphors, "the 'is' is both a literal 'is not' and a metaphorical 'is like.' "

6. See Barbour, *Myths, Models, and Paradigms*, pp. 13–14.

7. "El Shaddai," a name of God in the Hebrew Bible commonly translated "God Almighty," may also point to a female image. Wijk-Bos, *Reimagining God*, p. 27, suggests that its likely linguistic root is "breasted God."

8. McFague, *Models of God*, p. 34, succinctly states the relationship between models and metaphors: "A model is a metaphor with 'staying power.' " See also her comment about the importance of metaphors on p. 65: "If metaphors matter, then one must take them seriously at the level at which they function, that is, at the level of the imaginative picture of God and the world they project."

9. Following Sallie McFague and others. See McFague, *Models of God*, especially pp. 63–69. See also her *The Body of God: An Ecological Theology* (Minneapolis: Fortress, 1993), pp. 138–39. Jurgen Moltmann, *The Trinity and the Kingdom of God* (San Francisco: Harper & Row, 1981), refers to this model as "monarchical monotheism." Ian Barbour, *Myths, Models, and Paradigms*, pp. 155–57, 165–66, and *Religion in an Age of Science* (San Francisco: HarperSanFrancisco, 1990), pp. 244–47, summarizes the model and some of its problems.

10. I reduce the number of models to two contrasting alternatives for heuristic reasons, even as I am aware that a case could be made for multiple models (see, for example, Barbour, *Myths, Models, and Paradigms*, pp. 155–65, who describes five models). McFague in *Models of God* also speaks primarily of two models: she compares and contrasts the monarchical model with an alternative model built on the images of God as mother, lover, and friend. Dorothee Soelle, in her accessible and insightful *Theology for Skeptics: Reflections on God*, trans. by Joyce Irwin (Minneapolis: Fortress, 1995), also speaks of two sharply contrasting models, which she describes as authoritarian versus humanitarian (pp. 21–22), hierarchical versus liberationist (p. 25), subjection versus belonging (pp. 28–29); she associates the latter with mysticism, which she understands broadly as the authentic language of religion (pp. 43–44). Reducing alternatives to two is seen as simplistic by some. Walter Kaufmann, in the introduction to his translation of Buber's *I and Thou* (New York: Scribner's, 1970), pp. 9–18, implicitly criticizes Buber's reduction of our ways of being to two, I-You and I-It (see Chapter Two in this book). He argues that we in fact have multiple ways of being, and lists I-I, I-It, It-It, We-We, and Us-Them, as well as several modes of I-You. I for one am grateful that Buber spoke of two and not seven, eight, or nine.

11. Reflected, for example, in 2 Sam. 7.13–16 and Psalm 2.7.

12. For belief in an afterlife as a late development, see Chapter Seven, p. 157.

13. This can be seen in common English usage: first, to be merciful implies a situation of wrongdoing (one is merciful to somebody to whom one has the right to be otherwise); second, it implies a relationship of superior to subordinate. The Bible sometimes uses the term *mercy* or *merciful* in this sense, but sometimes the underlying Hebrew and Greek would be better represented in English by *compassion* or *compassionate*.

14. Ramshaw develops this phrase insightfully and powerfully in *God Beyond Gender*, Chapter Six, pp. 59–74.

15. McFague, *Models of God*, p. 63. Its images resound in the opening lines of Christian hymns familiar from my childhood: "Praise to the Lord the Almighty, the king of creation"; "Lead on, O King eternal, the day of march has come"; "God the omnipotent king who ordaineth"; "Dear Lord and Father of mankind, forgive our foolish ways." (About the last one, a participant in one of my workshops remarked, "There's enough political incorrectness to last a year.")

16. This is true unless the monarchical model is radically qualified and indeed subverted by the love of God; but then it essentially ceases to be the monarchical model.

17. Bondi, *Memories of God,* pp. 153–54. See also her memory of the three-point message of revival meetings: (1) "Each of us was so rotten to the core that we deserved to die and roast in hell forever"; (2) "God was enraged enough at us to kill us"; and finally, (3) "in spite of everything, God loved us enough to rescue us by sending his son as a sacrifice to die in our place" (p. 116). For her story of revisioning this notion, see her Chapter Four, pp. 111–44.

18. The phrase "stands over us" alludes to the suggestive German term that Freud used: the superego as *das Über-mich,* that which stands over me (in judgment).

19. Soelle, *Theology for Skeptics,* p. 24.

20. I owe the reference to Rev. Jan Griffin, associate rector of St. Mary the Virgin Episcopal Church in San Francisco, who got it from Anne Lamott, *Bird by Bird* (New York: Pantheon, 1994), p. 30.

21. I say "nearly universal" because some persons (such as narcissistic sociopaths) have little or no superego function.

22. Most emphatically by Jesus and Paul. The subversive wisdom of Jesus undermines the image of God as lawgiver and judge; see my *Meeting Jesus Again,* Chapter Four. Paul does the same thing with his subversion of "the law."

23. This is true of religions generally. Historically, the most common psychological effect of religion has been to reinforce superego function, both by declaring that society's laws (socialized into the superego) come from God and by invoking divine sanctions for nonobservance.

24. This is what I have elsewhere described as "Christian conventional wisdom"—namely, Christianity understood as a system of requirements and rewards. See *Meeting Jesus Again for the First Time,* pp. 75–80. The simple content of my childhood faith, "Believe in Jesus now for the sake of heaven later," is a classic example of Christian conventional wisdom.

25. The Bible and the Christian tradition contain another voice on this matter; my purpose here, however, is not to provide a comprehensive view of biblical and Christian perceptions of nature but to describe how the monarchical model addresses the issue.

26. McFague, *Models of God,* p. 66.

27. The classic "proof text" for this view is Gen. 1.26–28. The dominion of which it speaks is more limited than the way in which it is commonly understood: specifically, it is limited to dominion over living things (water creatures, air creatures, earth creatures); and verse 29 seems to imply that only plants are to be used for food. See also Psalm 8, esp. verses 5–8.

28. Our anthropocentric view of nature—our sense that we are at the center of things—is reminiscent of the pre-Copernican geocentric view of the universe, which literally placed the earth and humans at the center. Perhaps anthropocentrism is a psychological hangover. Although it is not the direct result of biblical teachings, it may be quite natural. To speculate: if cows had a creation story, no doubt they would be the climax of creation, and they might well see nature as there "for them."

29. See the famous essay by Lynn White, "The Historical Roots of Our Ecologic Crisis," *Science* 155 (1967): 1203–7. Although his essay has been criticized for being one-sided and not treating the diversity of biblical views of nature, it seems to me that White's central claim correctly identifies the effect of Christianity as mediated by the monarchical model. For a thoughtful treatment of connections between Christian theology and the ecological crisis, see Chapter Three of James A. Nash's *Loving Nature: Ecological Integrity and Christian Responsibility* (Nashville, TN: Abingdon Press, 1991), pp. 68–92.

30. The anthropocentric view of nature is also found in secular form and seems to be the dominant view in our culture. We see it whenever debates about the environment center primarily on the effects *on people* of environmental degradation and the economic cost of environmental protection.

31. Walter Wink, *Engaging the Powers* (Philadelphia: Fortress, 1992).

32. Mary Daly, *Beyond God the Father* (Boston: Beacon, 1973), p. 19.

33. This is not a matter of what is sometimes dismissively called political correctness. This demeaning phrase obscures a very important fact: language shapes perception and thought. It thus shapes our perceived reality, including the social structures and institutions that embody our shared perceptions and convictions. For a fine summary, see Anne E. Carr, *Transforming Grace: Christian Tradition and Women's Experience* (San Francisco: Harper & Row, 1988), pp. 134–44.

34. In addition to the works already cited, see the helpful compact annotated and categorized bibliography in Ramshaw, *God Beyond Gender*, citing books as recent as 1994.

35. Barbara Linder, a Lutheran pastor (ELCA) with whom I cotaught a course on Christian feminism about fifteen years ago.

36. Johnson, *She Who Is*, p. 83. Johnson also uses "Spirit" as the most comprehensive term for the sacred.

37. Johnson, *She Who Is*, p. 131. McFague, *Models of God*, pp. 169–71, suggests some problems with using "Spirit" as a model; for Johnson's response, see Johnson, *She Who Is*, p. 132. For McFague's own central use of Spirit, see *The Body of God*, esp. pp. 141–50.

38. See McFague's comment, *The Body of God*, p. 150: this model "radicalizes both divine immanence (God is the breath of each and every creature) and divine transcendence (God is the energy empowering the entire universe)."

39. Frequently found in the Psalms (for example, Ps. 42.9; 62.2, 6, 7; 73.26; 78.35; 92), it is also the dominant metaphor for God in Moses' "farewell address" in Deut. 32. See Wijk-Bos, *Reimagining God*, pp. 45–46.

40. The opening lines of a famous hymn express this well: "Rock of ages, cleft for me; let me hide myself in thee." Here God as rock becomes something one can be "in."

41. For God as mother, see esp. McFague, *Models of God*, pp. 97–123; Johnson, *She Who Is*, pp. 100–3, 170–87; Wijk-Bos, *Reimagining God*, pp. 50–65; Ramshaw, *God Beyond Gender*, pp. 105–7.

42. Respectively: Gen. 1.2, Isa. 43.13–14, Num. 11.11–12, Ps. 90.2, Deut. 32.18, Hos. 11.3–4, Isa. 66.13.

43. See esp. Phyllis Trible, *God and the Rhetoric of Sexuality* (Philadelphia: Fortress Press, 1978), Chapters Two and Three.

44. Soelle, *Theology for Skeptics*, pp. 22–25. She concludes (p. 25): "The father who is obsessed with his power, watches over it, and will not let anything be taken from him may be an end product of the social history of Christianity; but it has nothing in common with the use of the word in the Bible."

45. Because the significance of the Aramaic word *abba* as used by Jesus has sometimes been overstated or misunderstood, it is important to emphasize: (1) as a way of addressing God, the term within Judaism is not unique to Jesus (and thus does not point to a unique father-son relationship); and (2) it is not simply used by very young children to address their father—adult children also (then and now) use it. Nevertheless, it is quite different from addressing God as "king of the universe" or "Lord God Almighty."

46. Parental imagery for God (whether as mother or father) has limitations. My graduate assistant Mary Streufert observed that for many of us as adults, our parents are not the ones who know us best. Lovers or friends often know us better.

47. The wisdom woman is known as "Sophia" because "Sophia" is the Greek word for wisdom. For more extended treatments of Sophia, see Johnson, *She Who Is*, esp. pp. 86–100, 133–41; Kathleen M. O'Connor, *The Wisdom Literature* (Wilmington, DE: Michael Glazier, 1988), pp. 59–85; Wijk-Bos, *Reimagining God*, pp. 78–88; Roland E. Murphy, "Wisdom in the Old Testament," in *The Anchor Bible Dictionary*, ed. David Noel Freedman (New York: Doubleday, 1992), vol. 6, pp. 920–31, esp. pp. 926–27; Susan Cady, Marian Ronan, and Hal Taussig, *Sophia: The Future of Feminist Spirituality* (San Francisco: Harper & Row, 1986). For a compact introduction to Sophia and her connections to Jesus and the New Testament, see Chapter Five in my *Meeting Jesus Again*, pp. 96–118.

48. Important texts include Prov. 1.20–33, 3.13–19, 8.1–36 (esp. 22–31), 9.1–6; Wisdom of Solomon 7.22–8.1, 10.1–11.4; Ecclesiasticus (Sirach) 24.

49. Much as the *logos* ("Word") of the first chapter of John's gospel is. According to the first verse, the *logos*, or Word, is with God (implying a separate figure), yet the *logos* (Word) is God (implying identity). Indeed, much of what John says about *logos* applies equally well to Sophia; Sophia and *logos* seem to be functional equivalents.

50. See esp. Wisdom of Solomon 10.1–11.4, which retells the history of Israel, using *Sophia* instead of *God*.

51. Hos. 2 especially uses this image. Jeremiah a century later also uses the image, presumably independently of Hosea.

52. The Song of Songs (sometimes called the Song of Solomon) is a series of love poems describing passionate and erotic love between a man and woman. Whether its original meaning and use were religious is unclear.

53. There are also elements of male violence in the image; in Hosea and Jeremiah, God as lover threatens and enacts severe punishments on the adulterous beloved.

54. For God as lover, see especially McFague, *Models of God,* pp. 97–123, and Ramshaw, *God Beyond Gender,* pp. 102–5.

55. The most famous text is, of course, Ps. 23, with its familiar opening line: "The Lord is my shepherd."

56. If God is shepherd, we are sheep. The richness of the shepherd image is often lost because of an unfortunate tendency to see the sheep image negatively; it is often emphasized that sheep are really dumb or have gone astray. It thus becomes a primarily negative image of human beings. As an antidote, one might think of a shepherd carrying a sheep on his or her shoulders. Not only is this an image of closeness but it makes the point that sheep *matter* to a shepherd.

57. Paul Tillich, *Systematic Theology,* vol. 2 (Chicago: University of Chicago Press, 1957), pp. 244–75.

58. The phrase "sickness unto death" is from Soren Kierkegaard, *The Sickness Unto Death,* trans. Walter Lowrie (Princeton: Princeton University Press, 1941); refusing to be born comes from Hosea 13.13.

59. About this I will say more in Chapter Seven.

60. This will be the theme of Chapter Five.

61. Isa. 43.1–6.

CHAPTER 4

IMAGING GOD:

JESUS

AND GOD

Jesus is the image of the invisible God.[1]

We continue our exploration of imaging God by turning to Jesus. According to the New Testament, he is "the image of the invisible God,"[2] and the Christian message is "the gospel of the glory of Christ, who is the image of God"[3] As the image of God, Jesus discloses what God is like. He is an icon (to use the Greek word for image) through whom God is seen. As the image of the invisible God, Jesus is for Christians the decisive revelation of what God is like.

During the season of Epiphany in the weeks after Christmas each year, Christians celebrate Jesus as "the mystery of the Word made flesh" and thank God for having "caused a new light to shine in our hearts" by disclosing "your glory in the face of your Son Jesus Christ our Lord."[4] The metaphors are striking: in Jesus we see the Word made flesh, and in his face we see the glory of God. Jesus is thus the epiphany of God; the word *epiphany* means a manifestation "on the surface" of something from the depths. It is a strong claim: in Jesus we see what God is like.

To affirm that Jesus is the decisive revelation and disclosure of God need not imply that he is the only manifestation of God. Christians through the centuries have believed that the sacred has also been known elsewhere, notably in other major figures of the biblical tradition such as Moses, Elijah, and the prophets. Moreover, to many modern Christians (including me) it seems clear that manifestations of the sacred are also known in other religions in addition to Judaism and Christianity. So "decisive" does not mean "only." But for Christians, it does mean this: for us, here in the figure of Jesus is the decisive disclosure of what God is like.

JESUS AND GOD: WAS JESUS DIVINE?

Christians have said the most extraordinary things about Jesus. In writings that eventually became the New Testament, Jesus' followers in the first hundred years after his death spoke of him not only as the image of the invisible God but also as one with God, the glory of God, the Alpha and Omega, the only Son of God, the Wisdom of God, the Word become flesh, the bread of life, the firstborn of all creation, the true light that enlightens everyone, and more—this list is not comprehensive. In the early second century, the Christian bishop and martyr Ignatius referred to him simply as "our God, Jesus Christ." In the Nicene Creed of 325 C.E., the most important of the Christian creeds, Jesus is the second person of the Trinity. As such, he is very God of very God, light of light, coeternal with God ("begotten before all worlds"), and of one substance with God. Moreover, in much Christian worship and devotion, Jesus is praised as God and addressed in prayer as God.

Thus it is not surprising that Christians have frequently thought of Jesus as God. But was Jesus God? Is Jesus God? Or to use what may be a softer word, was Jesus divine? Is this an appropriate (or even the only appropriate) Christian way to speak of him?

Light is shed on the question of how we are to think about Jesus in relationship to God by the modern historical study of Jesus and Christian origins. Such study, beginning about two hundred years ago, is based on a fundamental distinction between two referents of the name "Jesus": the pre-Easter Jesus and the post-Easter Jesus.[5] They are quite different from each other, even while they are also related.

The pre-Easter Jesus is the historical Jesus. This Jesus is a figure of the past, a finite mortal human being born around the year 4 B.C.E. In his early thirties, after one to three years of public activity, he was executed by Roman authority (most likely in the year 30 C.E.). That Jesus —the flesh-and-blood Galilean Jewish peasant of the first century—is no more.[6]

The post-Easter Jesus is what Jesus became after his death. More specifically, the post-Easter Jesus is the Jesus of Christian tradition and experience (and both nouns are important). The post-Easter Jesus of Christian *tradition* is the Jesus of the developing traditions of early Christianity. The post-Easter Jesus includes the canonical Jesus (the Jesus we meet on the surface level of the New Testament) and the creedal Jesus (the Jesus of the classic Christian creeds of the 300s and 400s).

The post-Easter Jesus of Christian *experience* is the risen living Christ who was known after the death of the pre-Easter Jesus in the experience of his first followers and who continues to be known to this day. He is a figure of the present and not simply the past. Unlike the historical Jesus, he is not a mortal flesh-and-blood being, limited in time and space, in knowledge and power. Rather, he is a spiritual reality who is one with God and who has all of the qualities of God.

In this chapter, we will be concerned with both the pre-Easter and the post-Easter Jesus. What can be said about each of them? And as an epiphany and revelation of the sacred, as an image and icon of the invisible God, what does each disclose about God?

THE COMPOSITE JESUS OF CHILDHOOD: JESUS AS DIVINE

Until I began seminary, I was not aware of the distinction between the pre-Easter and post-Easter Jesus. Until then, I had combined everything I heard about him—from the New Testament, the creeds, hymns, sermons, and so forth—into what might be called "the composite Jesus." Much of that language said that he was divine. I therefore took it for granted that even as a historical figure, Jesus was God. To me, this meant that though Jesus had a body, had to eat and sleep, was born and died, and so forth, deep down he was really God.

Thus I thought that Jesus as a historical person (the pre-Easter Jesus) had the mind and power of God. That was how he could be the revelation of God. He knew things and spoke with divine authority because he had the mind of God, and he could do miracles because he had the power of God. I imagined that he was all-knowing: if you had asked him any question, he would have known the answer, whether it was about Einstein's theory of relativity or the capital of Kansas. I also imagined that he was all-powerful. Walking on water, feeding the multitude with a few loaves and a couple of fish, and raising Lazarus from the dead were pretty impressive. Matthew's addition to Mark's story of the arrest of Jesus made complete sense to me. According to Matthew, Jesus said, "Do you think that I cannot appeal to my Father, and he will at once send me more than twelve legions of angels?"[7] Yes, I thought, he could have.

The result was that Jesus as a historical figure basically ceased to be human (even though I knew that he was "true man" as well as "true God"). Instead, I thought of Jesus as God in human form. I now know that this is one of the earliest and most widespread Christian heresies, called "Docetism" (pronounced DOH-sit-ism). With its Greek root meaning "to seem" or "to appear," Docetism affirms that though Jesus seemed or appeared to be human, he was really God. Though heretical, Docetism is thought by many inside and outside the church to be standard Christian belief. And so I thought. The line from a familiar Christmas carol said it clearly: "Veiled in flesh the Godhead see, hail incarnate deity."[8]

DISTINGUISHING BETWEEN THE PRE-EASTER AND POST-EASTER JESUS

But the distinction between the pre-Easter Jesus and post-Easter Jesus that I learned in seminary leads to a different way of seeing the relationship between Jesus and God. The distinction is very illuminating.

The Christian theological tradition through the centuries has always been aware of such a distinction. But the understanding of the gospels that has emerged in the last two hundred years of biblical scholarship has sharpened our sense of the difference. Namely, the gospels of the New Testament (all composed in the last third of the first century) are the developing traditions of the early Christian communities in which they were written. As such, they contain two kinds of material: some goes back to Jesus as a figure of history, and some is the product of the communities themselves in the decades after Easter. To use an archaeological metaphor, they contain early layers and later layers.

The gospels are thus about both the pre-Easter Jesus and the post-Easter Jesus. That is, they contain some material that may be traced back to the pre-Easter Jesus, even while they are, in their present form, about the post-Easter Jesus of the developing Christian tradition. They include the community's memories of the pre-Easter Jesus, but these memories are seen through the lens and within the framework of their post-Easter convictions about Jesus. These memories are closest to the surface in the early layers of the synoptic gospels (Mark, Matthew, and Luke) and furthest removed in the gospel of John (which is dominated by post-Easter language about Jesus).[9] Thus, as historical sources, the gospels have early and late layers and are about *both* the pre-Easter Jesus and the post-Easter Jesus. They contain the community's memory of the pre-Easter Jesus and their testimony to the post-Easter Jesus.

When we separate the early layers of the tradition from later layers, an important result occurs. Statements in which Jesus affirms an exalted status for himself are not found in the earliest layers. What are sometimes called the exalted titles of Jesus (Jesus as messiah, Son of God, and so forth) disappear, as do statements such as "I and the father are one." These belong to later layers of tradition and express the community's post-Easter perceptions of and convictions about Jesus. They are thus not part of the pre-Easter Jesus' teaching.[10] This does not make them wrong; they accurately portray what Jesus became in the experience and tradition of early Christian communities after Easter. But the historical Jesus did not speak about himself using these categories.

Thus we begin with one of the most important results of modern Jesus scholarship: Jesus did not speak of himself (and apparently did not think of himself) as divine. So was the pre-Easter Jesus God? Was he divine? Apparently not in any sense of which he and his followers were aware.

The Pre-Easter Jesus

We will return soon to the question of how we might think of the pre-Easter Jesus' relationship to God. But first, what was he like? What can be said about the historical Jesus? A response to these questions intrinsically involves historical reconstruction. Constructing an image of the pre-Easter Jesus involves separating the gospel traditions into early and later layers[11] and then answering the question: What gestalt of Jesus—what overall sketch—best accounts for what we find in the earliest layers of the developing gospel tradition?

Diverse answers are given to this question, as the history and current status of the scholarly quest for the historical Jesus shows.[12] Here I will summarize the gestalt of Jesus that makes most sense to me. Because I have written extensively about this and do not wish to repeat myself too much, I will present three compact summaries of what I think we can know with a reasonable degree of probability about the pre-Easter Jesus.[13] All are versions of the same overall sketch.

But first an important prologue. Jesus was a deeply Jewish figure. This is a crucial awareness because of the tragic and sometimes murderous history of Christian anti-Judaism. Christians have often set Jesus in opposition to Judaism. Jesus is commonly seen as the founder of a new religion (Christianity) that was to replace Judaism (presumably because there was something wrong with it). "The Jews" are frequently spoken of as those who rejected Jesus and ultimately as those who were responsible for his death.[14]

But this is not the way it was. Historically speaking, "the Jews" did not reject Jesus. Responsibility for his execution rests with Roman authority and a narrow circle of the Jewish ruling elites who, far from representing the Jewish people, are better understood as the oppressors of the vast majority of the Jewish people in the first century.[15]

That Jesus was deeply Jewish does not mean simply that he was born Jewish. He grew up within the Jewish tradition, remained Jewish all his life, and saw himself as doing something within Judaism. He did not see himself as replacing Judaism or founding a new religion. Moreover, his early followers were all Jewish, as were all of the authors of the New Testament.[16] Jesus must be understood as a Jewish figure teaching and acting within Judaism; otherwise, we misunderstand him.

My first summary is a very compact version of the five-stroke sketch of Jesus I have described in other books. It reflects my cross-cultural approach to the study of religion in general and of Jesus and Christian origins in particular. Each stroke is a religious personality type known in many religious traditions, including the Jewish tradition. This approach, it seems to me, produces a reasonably comprehensive gestalt of the historical Jesus.

1. Jesus was a "Spirit person"—my phrase for a person who has frequent and vivid experiences of the sacred, of God, of the Spirit. He is similar to other Spirit persons in the Jewish tradition, for whom the sacred was an experiential reality: Moses, Elijah, the prophets. This seems to me the foundation of everything else he was.

2. Jesus was a healer. The evidence that he performed paranormal healings (as some Spirit persons do) is very strong. More healing stories are told about him than about any other figure in the Jewish tradition.

3. Jesus was a wisdom teacher. Using provocative short sayings (aphorisms) and memorable stories (parables), Jesus (like Lao-tzu, the Buddha, and Socrates, though in a very different style) taught an enlightenment wisdom flowing out of his experience of the sacred. Jesus spoke differently because he had seen differently.

4. Jesus was a social prophet. Like the God-intoxicated social prophets of the Hebrew Bible (Amos, Micah, Jeremiah, and so on), he challenged the domination system of his day, an oppressive social order with sharp social boundaries ruled over by a small class of urban elites. Moreover, he had an alternative social vision grounded in the compassion of God.[17]

5. Finally, Jesus was a movement initiator. A movement (at least in embryonic form—his public activity was very brief) came into existence around him during his lifetime whose inclusiveness and egalitarian practice embodied his alternative social vision.

My second summary puts this sketch into a one-minute-and-fifteen-second "sound bite," prepared for a mixed audience of Christians and non-Christians.[18] What does one say about the historical Jesus to such an audience in seventy-five seconds? I came up with:

Jesus was a peasant—which tells us about his social class.[19]

Clearly, he was brilliant. His use of language was remarkable and poetic, filled with images and stories. He had a metaphoric mind.

He was not an ascetic but world-affirming, with a zest for life.

There was a sociopolitical passion to him; like a Gandhi or a Martin Luther King Jr., he challenged the domination system of his day.

He was a religious ecstatic—a Jewish mystic, if you will—for whom God was an experiential reality. As such, he was also a healer. And there seems to have been a spiritual presence around him, like that reported of Saint Francis or the Dalai Lama.

And I suggest that as a figure of history, he was an ambiguous figure—you could experience him and conclude that he was insane, as his family did, or that he was simply eccentric, or that he was a dangerous threat—or you could conclude that he was filled with the Spirit of God.

My third summary is even more compact. It reduces what was most central to the pre-Easter Jesus to two parallel sets of three phrases:

There was a spirit dimension to Jesus, a wisdom dimension, and a political dimension.

Jesus was a Jewish mystic and healer, an enlightened wisdom teacher, and a social prophet.[20]

THE PRE-EASTER JESUS AND GOD

So what was the relationship of the pre-Easter Jesus to God? How might we think of it? As already noted, he did not speak of himself with the exalted titles that later layers of the tradition use. Moreover, there is reason to think he would have been shocked at the suggestion that he was divine. On one occasion, he even objected to being called "good": "Why do you call me good? No one is good but God alone."[21]

And yet I think there are historical grounds for speaking of the pre-Easter Jesus as one in whom the Spirit of God was experienced as present. The claim clearly reflects an early and widespread perception within Christian communities: they spoke of Jesus as one who had experiences of the Spirit, as one anointed by the Spirit, and as one in whom the Spirit of God was at work (explicitly in his teaching and healing).[22] Moreover, my strong hunch is that this was not simply a post-Easter impression of him. I think his followers during his lifetime sometimes experienced him as one in whom the Spirit was present.[23]

In my judgment, this was also most likely the experience of Jesus himself: he sometimes experienced the Spirit "around" or "in" or "on" him.[24] I do not mean that he would have spoken of it this way; he may or may not have. But I do mean that the community's estimate of him as anointed by the Spirit reflects not simply their own experience but also his. My basis for saying so is my claim that he was a Jewish mystic, a religious ecstatic, a "Spirit person." For whatever combination of reasons (genetic disposition, socialization, experience, and spiritual practices), his psyche seems to have been unusually open to the Spirit—to such an extent that the Spirit could be present in him or flow through him.[25] I do not think that he was filled with the Spirit or transparent to the Spirit from birth onward, or even that he was continuously so as the adult of his public activity. No doubt there were times when he experienced himself, and others experienced him, as quite ordinary. I think he got tired and had bad days. But I also think there were times when he experienced himself as a person in touch with the Spirit.

So, what was Jesus' relationship to God? In light of this sketch, a response requires two parts. Was the pre-Easter Jesus divine? No. But he was, according to those who followed him, one who knew the Spirit of

God and one in whom they experienced the presence of the Spirit. Is the post-Easter Jesus divine? Yes—the post-Easter Jesus of Christian experience and fully developed Christian doctrine is divine.[26] To that figure we now turn.

The Post-Easter Jesus

After his death, Jesus the Galilean Jew became in the experience and language of his followers "the face of God" and ultimately the second person of the Trinity. How and why did this happen? I see it as a three-fold process beginning with experience and moving through metaphorical expression to conceptual formulation.[27]

THE POST-EASTER JESUS OF CHRISTIAN EXPERIENCE

In the beginning was experience. The primary cause of the transition from the pre-Easter Jesus to the post-Easter Jesus was the experience of the community—more specifically, the *Easter* experience. The early Christian conviction that "God raised Jesus from the dead" is so widespread in the New Testament that it has been called "the earliest Christian creed."[28] That conviction was grounded in their experience of the risen Christ, and it gave birth to the post-Easter Jesus.

Though we celebrate Easter on a particular day, we should not think of the Easter experience of Jesus' early followers as happening on a single day or even over a period of forty days.[29] Rather, the phrase "the Easter experience" refers to the firsthand experience of Jesus as a living spiritual reality after his death. Easter experiences have continued through the centuries and into our own time.

This expansive meaning of Easter as the experience of the living spiritual Christ is pointed to by Paul's letters, the earliest writings to refer to the resurrection of Jesus (and the earliest writings in the New Testament).[30] In 1 Corinthians, written to a Christian community in Greece in the 50s, Paul says, "I have seen Jesus our Lord."[31] When did that happen? Paul had not seen the historical Jesus; he therefore was referring to the risen Christ. But when did Paul see the risen Christ?

Not until at least a few years after the death of Jesus, in what is commonly known as Paul's "Damascus Road" experience, described three times in the book of Acts. This experience was a vision, complete with a "photism" and "audition."[32] In 1 Corinthians 15, where Paul includes himself in a list of those to whom the risen Christ appeared, his language also suggests a visionary experience.[33] Moreover, in the rest of the chapter, Paul insists that the resurrection body is not a physical body but a spiritual body.[34] Thus Paul's "Easter experience" was the ecstatic (visionary) experience of the risen spiritual Christ some years after the death of Jesus.

We do not know whether the resurrection of Jesus involved an empty tomb or something happening to his physical body. Of course, if we read the resurrection stories in the gospels literally, it did. According to the earliest gospel Mark (written around 70), the tomb of Jesus was empty.[35] Moreover, the stories about the risen Jesus in the other gospels sometimes imply a quite physical reality: Jesus eats, invites Thomas to touch him, and cooks breakfast.[36] Yet it is not clear that we should read these stories literally—that is, as reporting the kinds of events that could have been experienced by a disinterested observer (or, as I sometimes put it, the kinds of events that could have been videotaped). The stories themselves contain "signals" that suggest that we are dealing with nonordinary reality and nonordinary perception: we are told that the risen Christ passed through walls, that his followers sometimes did not recognize him, and that it was possible to see him but still doubt.[37]

Nor does it seem to matter whether the Easter experience involved something happening to the corpse of Jesus, once the distinction between two often-confused words is seen. "Resuscitation" intrinsically involves something happening to a corpse; a person dead or believed to be dead comes back to life, resumes the conditions of physical existence, and will die again someday. "Resurrection" does not mean resumption of previous existence but entry into a different kind of existence. To use Paul's phrase, it involves a "spiritual body" (not a body of flesh and blood); moreover, a resurrected person will not die again. Resurrection *could* involve something happening to a corpse (transformation of some kind), but it need not.[38]

Thus Easter need not involve the claim that God supernaturally intervened to raise the corpse of Jesus from the tomb.[39] Rather, the core meaning of Easter is that Jesus continued to be experienced after his death, but in a radically new way: as a spiritual and divine reality. He was known in nonordinary experiences, as well as in the community's life together. The truth of Easter is grounded in such experiences of the risen Christ as a living presence,[40] not in physically observable events restricted to a particular day or a few weeks in the first century.

A second closely related factor contributing to the birth of the post-Easter Jesus is also experiential: the experience of the Spirit in early Christian communities. Early in the book of Acts, the community at Pentecost experienced the Spirit as tongues of fire and a great rushing wind.[41] The rest of the book of Acts as well as Paul's letters portray Spirit-filled communities in which ecstatic experiences were common. These experiences were linked to Jesus, though the terminology for doing so was still fluid. Sometimes the risen Jesus is spoken of as the giver of the Spirit; sometimes the Spirit is spoken of as the Spirit of Jesus, or the Spirit of Christ; and sometimes Spirit, God, and Christ seem to be used interchangeably. Such fluidity of terminology is not surprising in the early decades of a new religious movement. Behind the fluidity lies a common conviction, however: the experience of the Spirit was understood as the abiding presence of Jesus.

The experience of the risen Christ had two immediate implications. First, it was understood as God's vindication of Jesus. It meant that God had said "yes" to the pre-Easter Jesus—his message, activity, and vision. Just as the execution of Jesus was the domination system's "no" to Jesus, so the resurrection was God's affirmation of what had begun in Jesus.

Second, they spoke of Jesus as now being "at God's right hand." As a metaphor, the right hand of God is a position of honor, power, and authority. To say that Jesus had been "raised to God's right hand" meant that Jesus had been raised to divine status.[42] The "exaltation" of Jesus (as it is sometimes called) meant that Jesus was not seen simply as a hero who had been granted life after death in another realm; rather, it meant that he now participated in the power and authority of God. Thus the Easter experience meant not simply that Jesus was a living reality but also that he was now Lord. Put most compactly, Easter meant (and means): Jesus lives and is Lord.

METAPHORICAL AND CONCEPTUAL DEVELOPMENT

The Easter experience (with its twofold conviction that Jesus lives and is Lord) led to a transformed perception of Jesus among his followers. It generated a process of metaphorical and conceptual development that led to "the canonical Jesus" (the Jesus of the New Testament) and "the creedal Jesus" (the developed Christian doctrinal formulation of the fourth century).

During the hundred years after Jesus' death in which the traditions now found in the New Testament took shape, Christian communities used a large number of metaphors or images (mostly drawn from the Hebrew Bible) to speak about Jesus and his significance. Jesus was the servant of God, lamb of God, light of the world, bread of life, lord, door, vine, shepherd, messiah, savior, great high priest, sacrifice, Son of God, Wisdom of God, and Word of God. Over time, these metaphors became the subject of intellectual reflection and conceptualization. Some of this, ultimately, became doctrine. This whole process—from experience through metaphor to concepts and doctrine—is what I mean by "metaphorical and conceptual development." The process produced the post-Easter Jesus of Christian tradition.

To illustrate this process, I will summarize what I have written about elsewhere: two of the most important metaphors that emerged within the community for speaking about Jesus' relationship to God were Jesus as the Wisdom (or Sophia) of God and Jesus as the Son of God.[43] The use of Wisdom/Sophia imagery to speak of Jesus is widespread in earliest Christianity. It may have been the movement's earliest Christology (that is, its earliest way of talking about Jesus' relationship to God).[44] Central to Paul and John, it is also found in the synoptics. Jesus is spoken of as the child, prophet, and incarnation of divine Wisdom/Sophia. Moreover, because Wisdom/Sophia was with God from the beginning, the connection to Jesus leads to the claim that what was present in Jesus was coeternal with God. The language is incarnational.

Even more important in subsequent Christian history has been the metaphor of Jesus as the Son of God. Tracing its development is illuminating. In the Jewish tradition, "son of God" could refer to Israel, the king, angels, or Jewish Spirit persons.[45] It was a relational metaphor, pointing to an intimate relationship with God, like that of beloved child to parent. This seems its initial meaning as applied to Jesus: an affirmation that Jesus stood in an intimate relationship with God. Then it became a biological metaphor in the birth stories: God as the father of Jesus meant that Jesus did not have a human father but was conceived by the Spirit. Ultimately, it became a metaphysical or ontological claim: Jesus as the only begotten Son of God is of one substance with God. Something like this seems to have been the process by which the early community moved from the Easter experience through metaphor to fully developed post-Easter claims about Jesus as the preexistent Wisdom/ Sophia of God and coeternal Son of God.

The Post-Easter Jesus: The Canonical Jesus   This process of development can also be seen by looking at the canonical Jesus and the creedal Jesus. As mentioned earlier, the canonical Jesus is the Jesus we meet on the surface level of the gospels and the New Testament as a whole. The canonical Jesus includes Mark's Jesus, Matthew's Jesus, Luke's Jesus, Paul's Jesus, John's Jesus, and so forth. The canonical Jesus consists of the community's developing traditions about Jesus crystallized into writing at various points in time.

The canonical Jesus of the synoptic gospels is still more human than divine. Though at times portrayed as having extraordinary powers (walking on the sea, multiplying loaves), neither he nor his followers speak publicly about an exalted status during his lifetime. Instead, his identity is revealed in private epiphanies: to him at his baptism, to his inner circle of followers at his transfiguration, and in Peter's affirmation (also in private) at Caesarea Philippi: "You are the Christ."[46]

On the other hand, the Jesus of John's gospel is more divine than human. He repeatedly and publicly proclaims his divine identity: the Father and I are one; whoever has seen me has seen God. There are the great "I am" statements: I am the light of the world; the bread of life; the resurrection and the life; the way, the truth, and the life; the true vine; and so forth. Even the people arresting him recognize his divine status: when they tell him they are looking for Jesus of Nazareth, he says, "I am he" (one of the names of God), and they fall down in awe.[47] Strikingly, there is no story of his baptism or baptismal vision (even though his relationship to John the Baptizer is reported) and no story of the transfiguration in John. John has no need of particular epiphanies, for his whole gospel is an epiphany.

John's portrait of Jesus should not be dismissed as a historical falsification, however. His claims about Jesus come out of his community's experience of the post-Easter Jesus. In their experience, Jesus had become the light that enlightened them, the spiritual bread that fed them in the midst of their journey, the way that led them from death to life, and so forth. We understand the Johannine "I am" statements best when we hear them not as first-person declarations made by the pre-Easter Jesus but as third-person statements about the post-Easter Jesus: Jesus is the light of the world; Jesus is the bread of life; Jesus is the way, the resurrection, and the life. The Jesus of John's gospel speaks about what the post-Easter Jesus had become in the life of the Johannine community.

The Post-Easter Jesus: The Creedal Jesus   The canonical Jesus—the Jesus of the New Testament—became within another two hundred years the creedal Jesus. The process comes to fully developed conceptual and doctrinal expression in the Nicene Creed of 325 C.E. The creed is the indigenization of early Christian beliefs into the metaphysical categories of fourth-century Hellenistic philosophy. That is, the creed uses philosophical concepts such as "substance" and "person," which were current in that time. In it, Jesus is now fully divine, "one substance" with God (even as his humanity is still affirmed). The Trinitarian pattern of the creed (the first section is about God as creator, the second about Jesus, and the third about the Holy Spirit) integrates Jesus into the doctrine of the Trinity. The section about Jesus reads:

> We believe in one Lord, Jesus Christ, the only Son of God, eternally begotten of the Father, God from God, Light from Light, true God from true God, begotten, not made, of one Being [substance] with the Father. Through him all things were made. For us and for our salvation he came down from heaven; by the power of the Holy Spirit he became incarnate from the Virgin Mary, and was made man. For our sake he was crucified under Pontius Pilate; he suffered death and was buried. On the third day he rose again in accordance with the Scriptures; he ascended into heaven and is seated at the right hand of the Father. He will come again to judge the living and the dead, and his kingdom will have no end.

Thus, in the Nicene Creed, Jesus is the second person of the Trinity. My scholarly expertise does not extend into the fourth century, and there is much about the doctrine of the Trinity I do not pretend to understand.[48] But minimally, three meanings (appropriately) seem clear to me.

First, the Trinity affirms what Christian experience and devotion know: that the post-Easter Jesus—the risen living Christ—is a divine reality.

Second, the doctrine of the Trinity seeks to resolve an intellectual problem flowing out of that experience and devotion. Namely, how can one reconcile Christian post-Easter experience of Jesus as divine with monotheism? Does not that experience suggest that after Easter, there are now two divine realities, Jesus and God, rather than one? The doctrine of the Trinity says "no." The notion of one God in three persons seeks to preserve monotheism.

To understand this, we need to realize that the Latin and Greek words translated as "person" do not mean what "person" most commonly means in modern English. For us, "person" suggests a separate being (and thus suggests to many people that the Trinity is like a committee of three separate beings). But "person" in the ancient texts refers to the mask worn by actors in Greek and Roman theaters. Masks were not for concealment but corresponded to roles.

To speak of one God and three persons is to say that God is known to us wearing three different "masks"—in other words, in three different roles. The experiential meaning of the Trinity is actually quite simple: God is one and known to us in three primary ways. One of these ways—one of these roles or masks or faces—is Jesus. Jesus is the image of God and the face of God.[49]

Third, though the Trinity grows out of the post-Easter experience of Jesus as divine, it also makes an affirmation about the pre-Easter Jesus. Namely, it affirms that the pre-Easter Jesus was the incarnation of God. It does so in an interesting way: the Nicene Creed moves directly from Jesus' birth to his death and resurrection. It says nothing about his historical life between its beginning and its end. In this sense, the creed has a missing center. This need not be a defect, however, but can be seen as a clue to the purpose of the creed. Its purpose is not to affirm details about Jesus' life. Rather, by framing Jesus' life in this way, the creed affirms that Jesus was "of God" and that what happened in him was "of God." He was the incarnation of the Spirit.[50]

Trinitarian theology as expressed in the creed thus makes affirmations about both the post-Easter Jesus and the pre-Easter Jesus. It speaks of the risen living Christ as one with God and as the face of God: the post-Easter Jesus is God known in the face of Jesus. And it affirms that Jesus the Galilean Jew was, already in his historical life, the embodiment of the Spirit. Thus both the post-Easter Jesus and the pre-Easter Jesus are the image and face of the invisible God. Both are disclosures of the sacred.

THE PRE-EASTER JESUS AS A DISCLOSURE OF THE SACRED

If we take the pre-Easter Jesus seriously as an epiphany of God, as a revelation of the sacred, what do we see? What does he disclose about God, about the divine-human relationship, about the will of God? Based on my sketch of Jesus, I suggest the following:

First, Jesus disclosed that God can be known. For Jesus, and for the community around him, the Spirit was an experiential reality. God was not a distant reality who could only be believed in or who might be known only in the future or beyond death; rather, the Spirit is a presence "at hand." To use language from a previous chapter, the sacred is both immanent and transcendent.

Second, Jesus disclosed that the sacred is accessible apart from institutional mediation. In Jesus' social world, the official institutional mediator of the sacred was the temple in Jerusalem. Not only was the temple the place of God's presence but certain kinds of sins and impurities could be taken care of only through temple sacrifice. But Jesus (like his mentor John the Baptizer) affirmed the accessibility of God without temple mediation. He operated outside of institutional structures.[51]

Third, Jesus disclosed that God is compassionate. Jesus spoke of God that way: "Be compassionate, as God is compassionate."[52] Compassion is the primary quality of the central figures in two of his most famous parables: the father in the parable of the Prodigal Son and the Good Samaritan. And Jesus himself, as a manifestation of the sacred, is often spoken of as embodying compassion. As mentioned in the last chapter, to say that God is compassionate is to say that God is "womblike," not only as the source of life but as one who feels with and cares for the children of God's womb.

Fourth, Jesus disclosed that the divine-human relationship is not based on meeting requirements. We see this especially in his wisdom teaching.[53] Wisdom concerns the question "How shall I live?" Broadly speaking, wisdom comes in two forms: conventional and unconventional. Both are "ways" or "paths" of life. The former is a culture's established tradition about the way to live, sanctioned by the promise of reward and the threat of punishment. It is cultural consensus, "what everybody knows." One's status—in relation to tradition and in relation to God—depends on how well one measures up to standards of conventional wisdom. This is essentially what I called in the last chapter a "performance model" of the religious life.

Jesus was a teacher of unconventional wisdom—a culturally subversive wisdom that challenged conventional wisdom. As an enlightened teacher of an enlightenment wisdom, he sought to lead others to a new way of seeing. His aphorisms and parables functioned to invite a radical perceptual shift in how one sees life and God. Tradition-sanctioned statuses (of family, wealth, position, gender, righteousness) were subverted. Requirements were replaced by relationship as the central dynamic of the religious life. The way of Jesus was (and is) not about living within tradition and observing its requirements but about a new way of seeing. It is a vision of the religious life as a relationship to that which is beyond tradition.

The contrast between tradition and Spirit does not mean that tradition has no value or that it is always an obstacle. Rather, the indictment is against one way that tradition can function. Namely, when tradition is thought to state the way things really are, it becomes the director and judge of our lives; we are, in effect, imprisoned by it. On the other hand, tradition can be understood as a pointer to that which is beyond tradition: the sacred. Then it functions not as a prison but as a lens.

The alternative wisdom of Jesus—the way of Jesus—challenged the conventional wisdom not just of his world but of every world.[54] It involves a radical recentering: from being centered in our tradition—that is, in our map of reality, whether religious or secular—to being centered in that to which these maps (at their best) point. Life within tradition is transformed to life in the Spirit. The life of performance becomes the life of relationship.

Fifth, Jesus spoke and enacted a social vision grounded in God—what I will call "the dream of God" in Chapter Six. We see his social passion and vision in several ways: in his role as a social prophet who indicted the ruling elites at the top of an exploitative domination system; in his boundary-breaking behavior and in the inclusive shape of his movement, which undermined the sharp social boundaries of his day; in his inclusive table fellowship, his practice of "open commensality," which embodied his inclusive social vision. We see it also in his frequent use of the phrase "kingdom of God," at least one of whose meanings is social and political. The contrast is to the kingdom of Herod and the kingdom of Caesar: What would the world be like if God were king and not Herod or Caesar?[55] This is a very different vision. There is thus a social-political dimension to Jesus, and if we see Jesus as a disclosure of God, it follows that God cares passionately about what happens in human history.

Cumulatively, taking the pre-Easter Jesus seriously as an epiphany of God suggests a massive subversion of the monarchical model of God and the way of life (individually and socially) to which it leads. God is not a distant being but is near at hand. God is not primarily a lawgiver and judge but the compassionate one. The religious life is not about requirements but about relationship. God as king has not ordained a social order dominated by earthly kings and elites but wills an egalitarian and just social order that subverts all domination systems. Indeed, Jesus used the monarchical language of "kingdom of God" to subvert the monarchical model: in the kingdom of God, things are very different.

THE CANONICAL JESUS AS A DISCLOSURE OF GOD

Speaking at length about the canonical Jesus as a disclosure of God is impossible in the concluding pages of this chapter. Individual stories in the gospels are disclosures, and each gospel as a whole is a disclosure, as is what the other writers of the New Testament say about Jesus. Instead I will focus on what might be called the completed canonical story of Jesus: what happens when the story of Jesus is put within the framework of the canonical stories about the beginning and ending of his life. In short I will focus on the stories of his birth, death, and resurrection and the way they generate the classic Christian story of Jesus as a disclosure of God.

To do so, I will use the term *myth*. Using this term requires a strong warning against a common misunderstanding of the word. For many people in the modern world, *myth* is a dismissive term. In popular usage, myth most often means an untruth that need not and should not be taken seriously. Thus for many Christians, speaking of biblical stories as "myths" is unsettling or even inflammatory. This is unfortunate, for myth has a very different meaning in the study of religion. It is a very useful and illuminating term. Religious myths or sacred myths are stories about the relationship between the two worlds—the sacred and the world of our ordinary experience. In short, a myth is a story about God and us. As such, myths can be both true and powerful, even though they are symbolic narratives and not straightforward historical reports. Though not literally true, they can be really true; though not factually true, they can be actually true.

The stories of Jesus' birth are myths in this sense. Along with most mainline scholars, I do not think these stories report what happened.

The virginal conception, the star, the wise men, the birth in Bethlehem where there was no room in the inn, and so forth are not facts of history. But I think these stories are powerfully true. They make use of rich archetypal religious images and motifs to speak of Jesus' significance. The star shining in the night sky and the wise men following the star suggest that the story of Jesus is the story of light coming into the darkness. As John's gospel (which has no birth story) puts it, "the true light that enlightens every person was coming into the world." The birth stories are a tale of two lordships and of the conflict and choice between the kingdoms of this world and the kingdom of God. There is the lordship of Herod and Caesar, and there is the lordship of Jesus. The story of conception by the Spirit affirms that what happened in Jesus was of God.

The stories of Jesus' death and resurrection contain a mixture of historical memory and mythical narration. The stories of Jesus' execution are closer to history than are the birth stories: he really was crucified under Pontius Pilate around the year 30. Moreover, he died as a martyr and not a victim; a martyr is executed because he or she stands for something, whereas a victim is simply in the wrong place at the wrong time. Jesus was killed by the domination system because of what he stood for.

But as the stories of Jesus' death and resurrection are told, the authors of the New Testament make use of a number of symbolic motifs to suggest its religious significance.[56] I will mention three. Within the framework of what is called the "Christus Victor" motif, Jesus' death and resurrection are the defeat of the principalities and powers, all those forces of bondage that enslave us. Through the cross, "he disarmed the rulers and authorities and made a public example of them, triumphing over them in it."[57] Jesus' death and resurrection are also understood as a symbol and embodiment of the path of return to God: we die to an old way of being in order to be born into a new way of being. So Paul spoke of it: "I have been crucified with Christ; it is no longer I who live but Christ who lives in me."[58] Finally, Jesus' death is also understood with the symbolism of temple sacrifice. To say that Jesus is the once-and-for-all sacrifice for sins is to say that our sins have been taken care of.

The stories of the beginning and ending of Jesus' life thus have powerful individual themes. But I turn now to what happens when the story of Jesus as a whole is framed by the stories of Christmas, Good Friday, and Easter. The story as whole—the completed Christian story—becomes a story about God and us, a myth about God and us.

As myth, the story as a whole becomes a disclosure of God's involvement in our lives. Within the myth, Jesus is not simply a Jewish mystic, wisdom teacher, and social prophet but also the only begotten Son of God, conceived by the Spirit and born of a virgin. Thus the story of Jesus is the story of "God with us." The teaching of Jesus becomes the wisdom of God, the compassion of Jesus becomes the compassion of God, the social vision of Jesus becomes the dream of God.

The story of Jesus' passion takes on added meanings as well. The story of the Last Supper is simultaneously about the last meal shared by Jesus with his friends (if there was one) and also the story of God's only Son about to give up his life for the sake of the world and instituting a sacrament through which his followers may forever be nourished by his body and blood. The story of Jesus' suffering on the cross receives the added dimension of God participating in our suffering: God suffers with us. Moreover, seeing Jesus' death as the death of God's only Son discloses the depth of God's love for us. In the noninclusive language of the best known verse from my childhood: "For God so loved the world that he gave his only begotten Son to die for us."

Within the completed Christian myth as found in the canon, the story of Jesus is thus a story of God and us. This does not mean, of course, that the historical Jesus was God. But because the completed story affirms that God was present in and through Jesus, the story of Jesus becomes a disclosure of God, the revelation and epiphany of God.

As a disclosure of God, its cumulative effect is powerful. The story affirms that God wills our well-being: our liberation from that which enslaves us, our return from exile and estrangement, our acceptance in spite of our sense of unworthiness, our transformation from blindness and preoccupation to sight and compassion.

In the history of scholarship, theological reflection on the distinction between the pre-Easter Jesus and the canonical Jesus has often led to an unnecessary either-or choice: that *either* the historical Jesus *or* the canonical Jesus is of primary significance for the Christian life.[59] But this is an unnecessary choice. Both are significant. Our glimpses of the pre-Easter Jesus disclose what the Word made flesh, the Spirit of God embodied in a human life, looks like. The canonical Jesus discloses what Jesus became in the experience and life of early Christian communities.

We do not need to choose between them. Our understanding of Jesus' significance is richer if we see and affirm both the historical Jesus and the canonical Jesus. Both the pre-Easter Jesus and the post-Easter Jesus are the image of the invisible God. Both disclose what God is like.

Notes

1. Col. 1.15.
2. Col. 1.15.
3. 2 Cor. 4.4b.
4. Preface for Epiphany from the Episcopal *Book of Common Prayer.*
5. Sometimes also expressed as the distinction between "the Jesus of history" and "the Christ of faith."
6. Lest I be misunderstood here, I want to emphasize that this statement is not a denial of Easter, about which I shall say more later. Rather, I am making a very basic point: Jesus as a flesh-and-blood Galilean peasant (Jesus as a protoplasmic being) is not around anymore.
7. Matt. 26.53.
8. From the second verse of "Hark the Herald Angels Sing." It may be possible to give this line an orthodox meaning (though it's a stretch). I am simply reporting what it meant to me.
9. According to the most widely accepted scholarly view, the earliest of our present gospels is Mark (written around 70), which both Matthew and Luke used as a source when writing their gospels in the next two decades. The earliest written layer of the synoptic tradition is "Q," a collection of the sayings of Jesus involving about two hundred verses now found in Matthew and Luke and probably put into writing in the decade beginning with 50 C.E. For a recent reconstruction and translation of Q, see *The Lost Gospel Q,* ed. Marcus Borg, Mark Powelson, and Ray Riegert, intro. by Thomas Moore (Berkeley: Ulysses Press, 1996). John is probably the latest of the gospels, written near the year 100.
10. For discussion of relevant texts, see my *Jesus: A New Vision,* pp. 4–6, and n.6, pp. 17–18.
11. For compact summaries of this understanding of the gospels, see my *Jesus at 2000,* pp. 121–47; and *Jesus in Contemporary Scholarship,* pp. 160–81. For the most systematic development of this understanding, see John Dominic Crossan, *The Historical Jesus: The Life of a Mediterranean Jewish Peasant* (San Francisco: HarperSanFrancisco, 1991).
12. For the quest to 1900, the classic work is Albert Schweitzer, *The Quest of the Historical Jesus* (New York: Macmillan, 1968; originally published in 1906). For the current status of the quest, see my *Jesus in Contemporary Scholarship,* pp. 18–43; for a conservative-evangelical approach, see Ben Witherington III, *The Jesus Quest* (Downers Grove, IL: Intervarsity Press, 1995); for a strong critique of the quest, see Luke Johnson, *The Real Jesus* (San Francisco: HarperSanFrancisco, 1996).
13. See especially my *Jesus: A New Vision* and *Meeting Jesus Again for the First Time,* as well as *Jesus at 2000,* pp. 9–11.
14. Parts of the New Testament reinforce this notion. In his story of Jesus' trial, the author of Matthew adds a passage to his source (Mark) that makes the Jewish crowd responsible for the death of Jesus and even has them invoke a terrible curse on themselves: "His blood be upon us and our children!" (Matt. 27.25). The author of John frequently describes the enemies of Jesus simply as "the Jews." Yet neither author meant these words as commonly understood in later Christianity. Initially, they were part of an intra-Jewish conflict: Jews were speaking about other Jews. The authors of both Matthew and John were Jews who had become part of the Christian movement, and the communities for which they wrote were primarily Jewish-Christian. In their minds, they were not indicting all Jews but some Jews (namely, Jews who were opponents). In subsequent centuries, when most Christians were no longer of Jewish origin, these words became part of a malignant Christian stereotype of all Jews. When these texts are read without an awareness of their first-century setting and meaning, they become pervasively misleading and dangerous. This is a problem for the church, especially during Holy Week, when millions of Christians hear their sacred Scriptures denouncing "the Jews" as responsible for the death of Jesus.

15. On the stories of Jesus' death, see especially John Dominic Crossan, *Who Killed Jesus?* (San Francisco: HarperSanFrancisco, 1995).

16. The possible exception is the author of Luke and Acts, who may have been a Gentile.

17. That there is a strong political dynamic in Jesus' message and activity is an emphasis of much contemporary Jesus scholarship. For an overview, see Chapter Five in my *Jesus in Contemporary Scholarship*, pp. 97–126. See also Crossan's scholarly study *The Historical Jesus: The Life of a Mediterranean Jewish Peasant* and his popular *Jesus: A Revolutionary Biography* (San Francisco: HarperSanFrancisco, 1994), as well as Richard Horsley, *Jesus and the Spiral of Violence* (San Francisco: Harper & Row, 1987). For a compact compelling summary of Jesus' challenge to the domination system, see Walter Wink, *Engaging the Powers*, pp. 109–37. See also Chapter Six in this book.

18. One minute and fifteen seconds was the amount of time I was given on NBC's *Today Show* to respond to the question, "What was Jesus like?" For the story, see *Jesus at 2000*, pp. 9–10.

19. The peasant social class included not just agricultural workers but also artisans, fishers, and so forth. Jesus' father and Jesus himself may have been carpenters, which means that their family at some point had lost their land; they thus would have been more economically marginal than a peasant family that still owned a plot of land.

20. When pressed by a television interviewer to come up with a "sound-bite" summary of Jesus a few seconds long, John Dominic Crossan said, "He was a peasant with an attitude." Crossan is arguably the premier Jesus scholar in the world today. In addition to his best-selling but quite technical *The Historical Jesus* and *Who Killed Jesus?*, see his popular-level best-seller *Jesus: A Revolutionary Biography* (1994) and *The Essential Jesus* (1994), both published by HarperSanFrancisco. My perception of Jesus is quite similar to his, despite the fact that our angles of vision and much of our language are somewhat different.

21. Mark 10.17–18. It is interesting to note how Matthew changes this as he copies Mark: Matthew has Jesus say, "Why do you ask me about what is good?" (Matt. 19.17).

22. Though passages linking Jesus and the Spirit are especially frequent in Luke, the emphasis is not simply due to Luke; such passages are found in Q, Mark, and material peculiar to Matthew (as well as in John and Paul). Seeing Jesus as one in whom the Spirit of God was present and/or active was clearly a widespread and strong community perception.

23. According to both Mark and Q, even his opponents experienced him as a "Spirit person," but of the wrong kind.

24. For an extended treatment of Jesus and the Spirit, see my *Jesus: A New Vision*, pp. 39–75.

25. I suggest this not as a specific explanatory hypothesis but more generally as a way of thinking about the relationship between Jesus and the Spirit.

26. To clarify: my position here is not the same as "adoptionism," which affirms that Jesus was simply human during his life and then became divine after his death. Rather, my position affirms the presence of the Spirit in Jesus during his life. Thus there is continuity (as well as discontinuity) between the pre-Easter and post-Easter Jesus.

27. I also describe this process in my chapter, "From Galilean Jew to the Face of God: The Pre-Easter and Post-Easter Jesus," in *Jesus at 2000*, pp. 7–20.

28. James Dunn, "Christology (NT)," *Anchor Bible Dictionary*, vol. 1, p. 982. See Rom. 10.9, 1 Thess. 1.10, Rom. 8.11, Gal. 1.1, Col. 2.12, Eph. 1.20, 2 Tim. 2.8. The formula seems to be earlier than Paul.

29. The period of forty days between Easter and the ascension of Jesus into heaven is based on Acts 1.3, the only place in the New Testament that mentions a specific limited period of time during which Easter experiences occurred. That the author of Luke-Acts probably did not mean this literally is suggested by the fact that Luke 24.51 reports that Jesus ascended into heaven on the day of Easter itself, not forty days later. Either we need to suppose that the author did not notice this discrepancy in his own writing or that he did not see it as a contradiction. The latter seems more likely.

30. Paul's genuine letters (written between approximately 48 and 62 C.E.) are the oldest documents in the New Testament (earlier than all the gospels, written between 70 and 100, with Mark the earliest and John most likely the latest). Of the thirteen letters in the New Testament attributed to Paul, there is general scholarly agreement that three are not by him (the "pastoral letters" of

Titus, 1 and 2 Timothy); another three are disputed (Ephesians, Colossians, and 2 Thessalonians). The remaining seven are generally agreed to be genuine: Romans, 1 and 2 Corinthians, Galatians, Philippians, 1 Thessalonians, and Philemon.

31. 1 Cor. 9.1.

32. With differences in details in Acts 9, 22, and 26. A "photism" (common in visions) is an experience of light, an "audition" an experience of a voice.

33. 1 Cor. 15.3–8. The language of verse 8 ("Last of all, as to one untimely born, he appeared also to me") need not mean that Paul thought there was only a limited period of time during which the risen Christ appeared, with Paul's own experience as the last one there would be; rather, the words more naturally mean that Paul's experience is the last one he mentions in his list.

34. 1 Cor. 15.35–50. The section begins with the question, "With what kind of body are the dead raised?" The analogy Paul uses to talk about the relationship between the physical body and the spiritual resurrection body is instructive: it is like the relationship between a seed and a full-grown plant. The analogy affirms both continuity (the seed becomes the plant) and radical discontinuity (in appearance, seed and plant are radically different).

35. Mark 16.1–8. It is important to note that this is the first reference to an empty tomb; Paul does not mention it. Moreover, the way Mark tells the story has seemed to some scholars to suggest that the empty tomb story is a relatively late development: Mark tells us that the women who discovered the empty tomb *didn't tell anybody about it,* thereby explaining why this story was not widely known.

36. Luke 24.39–43; John 20.24–29, 21.9–14. It is interesting that Mark has no stories of the risen Christ appearing to his followers but only the story of the empty tomb. The other three gospels (all later) do have appearance stories, all different from each other. This is quite a change from the pre-Easter portions of the gospels, where there is considerable duplication and overlap. What to make of this difference is not clear.

37. Passing through walls (or materializing and dematerializing): John 20.19, 26; Luke 24.31, 36. Doubt even after seeing Jesus: Matt. 28.17. The classic "nonrecognition" story is the Emmaus Road story, Luke 24.13–35, in which two followers of Jesus journey with the risen Christ for several hours without recognizing him.

38. For further development of this point, see *Jesus at 2000,* pp. 13, 15–17.

39. Caution about the limits of our knowledge leads me to say that I cannot rule out that possibility, though for a variety of reasons I view it as remote. It also seems to me that many (not all) who stress that it did involve a supernatural intervention by God then use that claim to "prove" something about God, Jesus, and Christianity: that God intervened on a particular Sunday morning in Palestine in a way that God had never before or has not since done; that this proves that Jesus really was who he (allegedly) said that he was; that this proves the truth of Christianity and indeed proves its unique truth (for God has acted in this tradition as in no other). But the argument seems to ignore what the texts (especially Paul) actually say. It also seems backward: it begins with the claim that the Easter stories are factually true and then argues that you can therefore take God, Jesus, and Christianity seriously. But presumably taking God and Jesus seriously is the basis for being willing to take these stories seriously (even if not literally).

40. To clarify: I am saying more than simply that Jesus was remembered or that his spirit lived on (as we might speak of the spirit of Abraham Lincoln or Martin Luther King Jr. living on). I am convinced that people (then and now) really experienced Jesus as a living reality after his death.

41. Acts 2. I do not take this as straightforward historical reporting, but the narrative clearly reflects the community's sense of being a Spirit-filled community. It is interesting that one of the consequences of the coming of the Spirit was the overcoming of the fragmentation of the human community into diverse languages; it is a reversal of the Tower of Babel story (Gen. 11).

42. That Jesus was raised to God's right hand is an early way of talking about the resurrection of Jesus (see Acts 2.32–33, 7.55–56; Rom. 8.34; Eph. 1.20; Col. 3.1; Heb. 1.3, 8.1, 10.12, 12.2; 1 Pet. 3.22). Here the emphasis is not on raised *from the tomb* but on exaltation: Jesus raised (exalted or elevated) to God's right hand.

43. See *Meeting Jesus Again,* Chapter Five, and *Jesus at 2000,* pp. 13–15.

44. See, for example, Johnson, *She Who Is,* pp. 94–100, 156–67; Elisabeth Schüssler Fiorenza, *In Memory of Her* (New York: Crossroad, 1985), pp. 130–40, 188–92; James D. G. Dunn, *The Partings of the Ways* (Philadelphia: Trinity Press International, 1991), pp. 195–201.

45. Israel as God's son: Exod. 4.22, Hos. 11.1. The king as God's son: 2 Sam. 7.14, Ps. 2.7. Angels as sons of God: Job 1.6. Jewish religious ecstatics as sons of God: see Geza Vermes, *Jesus the Jew* (New York: Macmillan, 1973), pp. 210–13.

46. Mark 1.11, 9.2–8, 8.27–30.

47. John 18.4–6. This is, of course, impossible to imagine historically. Police do not acknowledge somebody to be divine and then arrest him or her anyway.

48. For further treatment of the Trinity, see Catherine Mowry LaCugna, ed., *Freeing Theology* (San Francisco: HarperSanFrancisco, 1993), pp. 83–114, and *God for Us: The Trinity and Christian Life* (San Francisco: HarperSanFrancisco, 1991); Johnson, *She Who Is,* pp. 191–223; Douglas John Hall, *Professing the Faith* (Minneapolis: Fortress, 1993), pp. 55–72.

49. My understanding is that the doctrine of the Trinity means more than this. That is, many theologians speak of the Trinity as referring not only to three primary ways in which God is known to us but also of internal relations within the Trinity. I do not yet understand this.

50. This affirmation is the same one made in the canonical portraits of Jesus. They portray him as the Word become flesh, as the Wisdom of God and Son of God, and as the incarnation of God. Though this language is the product of the community and not part of Jesus' self-understanding, it also expresses a conviction about the pre-Easter Jesus: he was "of God."

51. Crossan emphasizes that Jesus' activity as healer makes the same point: Jesus healed outside of institutional structures and thereby announced the immediacy of access to God and "the brokerless kingdom of God" (*The Historical Jesus,* p. 422).

52. Luke 6.36 (Q material). The close parallel in Matt. 5.48 speaks of God as "perfect" rather than compassionate, but this seems to reflect Matthew's editorial change.

53. For fuller development of this paragraph, see *Meeting Jesus Again,* Chapter Four.

54. I want to emphasize that the problem with the conventional wisdom that Jesus subverted was not its specific content (that is, that it simply had the wrong requirements). This way of seeing it usually leads to a negative impression of Judaism, as if the problem was that the tradition of Jesus' day was Jewish and needed to be replaced. When it is seen this way, the message of Jesus is turned into Christian conventional wisdom: Jesus replaced wrong beliefs with right beliefs or an inadequate set of requirements with the right set of requirements. The framework of conventional wisdom (including the dynamic of "measuring up") remains. But this is precisely the framework that Jesus subverts, and it applies equally to all forms of conventional wisdom, whether Jewish, Christian, or secular.

55. I owe this way of putting it to Crossan, "Jesus and the Kingdom" in Borg, ed., *Jesus at 2000,* pp. 33–34.

56. On this whole section, see especially Gustaf Aulen, *Christus Victor,* trans. A. G. Hebert (New York: Macmillan, 1969; originally published in 1931), as well as Chapter Six of my *Meeting Jesus Again.*

57. Col. 2.15.

58. Gal. 2.20.

59. See Luke Johnson's recent critique of Jesus scholarship, *The Real Jesus: The Misguided Quest for the Historical Jesus and the Truth of the Traditional Gospels* (San Francisco: HarperSanFrancisco, 1996). Johnson charges most of the rest of us with saying that only the historical Jesus matters and argues instead that only the canonical Jesus matters (which is what he means by "the real Jesus"). Not only does his charge seem unfair (some of us do not hold the position ascribed to us) but the either-or choice also seems ill advised. For my own treatment of the matter (published before Johnson's book), see *Jesus in Contemporary Scholarship,* Chapter Nine.

PART 3

LIVING
WITH
GOD

CHAPTER 5

OPENING

TO GOD:

THE HEART

OF SPIRITUALITY

One of the most important claims of this book is that God is all around us. The sacred is not "somewhere else," spatially distant from us. Rather, we live within God. The nonmonarchical images of God (and of Jesus as the disclosure of God) suggest that God has always been in relationship to us, journeying with us, and yearning to be known by us. Yet we commonly do not know this or experience this. In this chapter we will be concerned with why this is the case and even more with how this situation is remedied by "opening" to God.

We thus move to the very practical question of how religions (and Christianity in particular) function to bring about a transformation of the self; we will look at their role as a "means of ultimate transformation."[1] We will consider a large variety of traditional religious practices and their spiritual function or purpose: to mediate an opening of the self at its deepest level to the sacred and to bring about a recentering of the self in the God in whom we live and move and have our being. We will be centrally concerned with "spirituality," the internal dimension of the religious and Christian life.

WHY THE SACRED IS NOT MORE APPARENT

If God is all around us, why is the reality of God not more apparent to us? A number of evocative images and perceptive insights from ancient and modern times suggest answers. These images and insights are complementary and not competitive; no one of them is *the* reason. Rather, they are different angles of vision on the same problem, and each contributes to understanding it.

We live "east of Eden." This phrase from the early chapters of Genesis describes metaphorically a central feature of the human condition.[2] The Garden of Eden is a symbol for paradise, which means life in the manifest presence of God. Human life begins in Eden, in the presence of God, but something has happened so that we are no longer aware of that. Life in history is typically experienced as life outside the garden, life unaware of the presence of the sacred. We are estranged—separated from that to which we belong.

Why is that? One reason is that our five senses are most capable of experiencing the visible world of our ordinary experience. We live at an "epistemic distance" from God.[3] "Epistemic" is related to "epistemology," which concerns how we know. Although we are spatially close to God (for we are in God), we are epistemologically distant; our senses are geared to knowing one level of reality—namely the world of matter and energy, time and space. We are capable of perceiving more; as the nature mystic Loren Eiseley suggests, we humans are like the Brazilian amphibian fish whose eyes have two lenses, one for seeing under the water and one for seeing above the water.[4] But most of us most of the time have cataracts on our second lens. We commonly do not perceive the world of Spirit.

Saint Paul argues that our blindness flows from our centering in the finite rather than the infinite. We center our lives in the created rather than in the creator.[5] Why do we do that? Perhaps because the finite is most apparent to us; perhaps also because of a primal anxiety that leads us to seek security in what we can most readily grasp.

Our lack of awareness of the sacred is also to some extent the result of the socialization process through which we all go as we grow up. We are socialized into a world based on language, and language intrinsically categorizes and divides reality. To use Martin Buber's terminology, growing up involves socialization into the world of I-It.[6] The more successful our socialization, the deeper we are immersed and enmeshed in the world of I-It. The words and categories of culture shape and limit our perception, screening out the reality known in I-You moments.

Socialization in the modern period intensifies the problem. The central dynamic of modern Western culture focuses our attention on the finite. Paul Tillich called this cultural dynamic "the spirit of industrial society"—a way of living organized around production and consumption.[7] Our modern preoccupation with producing and consuming leads us to live on the surface level of reality and to seek our satisfaction in the finite. But the sacred is known in the depths of reality, not in the manipulation and consumption of the surface.

THE HEART

Thus a variety of factors contribute to our not being aware of the sacred, of God, as the encompassing reality all around us. The Bible uses several metaphors to image the resulting human condition.[8] One of its central metaphors is that we have "hard hearts." To understand the metaphor, we need to know that "heart" in the biblical tradition is an image for the self at its deepest level. For the ancient Hebrews, the heart was not simply associated with feelings or courage or love, as in common modern usage. Rather, the heart was associated with the totality of the human psyche: not only emotion but also intellect, volition, and even perception. As a level of the self "below" our feeling, thinking, willing, and seeing, the heart impacts all of them.

What matters is the condition of the heart. One can have a "hard heart" or a "soft heart." Each is part of a family of metaphors. A "hard heart" is also a "a heart made of stone," a heart that is "closed" and "shut," "a fat heart" enclosed in a thick layer, a heart that is "proud" and puffed up.[9] Or one can have "a soft heart," "a tender heart," "a heart made of flesh," "a broken heart."[10]

A hard heart is associated with sensory malfunction and intellectual incomprehension. A fat heart shuts the eyes, stops the ears, darkens the mind.[11] A hard heart is associated with not hearing, not seeing, not understanding, and not remembering.[12] A closed heart and shut eyes go together.[13] A proud heart goes with arrogance, with greed and strife, with "haughty eyes" that are "the lamp of the wicked," and with having forgotten God.[14] A hard heart does not know the sacred and has no sense of awe.[15] It is resistant to the voice and will of God, as in the stories of Pharaoh with his "hardened heart" refusing to let the Israelites leave

Egypt. It lacks compassion.[16] A hard heart goes astray, does not regard God's ways, and does not hear God's voice.[17] With hard hearts, we have eyes but do not see, ears but do not hear, minds but do not understand.

The cumulative effect of this imagery suggests both a diagnosis and a prescription for cure. Our problem—the reason we do not see God and the reason the reality of God is not more apparent to us—is that we have "hard hearts." It is as if we have a thick layer or rind around the self at its deepest level. Our hearts are encrusted. They are not typically soft, receptive, open.

What is needed is an open heart, a soft heart, a new heart. Ezekiel associated this with spirit: a new spirit turns a heart of stone into a heart of flesh.[18] So also the psalmist: "Create in me a clean heart, O God, and put a new and right spirit within me."[19] Jeremiah spoke of "a new covenant" to be "written on the heart" and consisting of *knowing* God:

> No longer shall they teach one another or say to each other, "Know the Lord," for *they shall all know me.*[20]

The new covenant—a new way of being in relationship with God replacing the old covenant of externals written on stone—is written on the heart and associated with knowing God.[21] New heart, new spirit, and knowing the sacred go together.

Thus the heart needs to be opened. To use a favorite metaphor, spirituality is "for the hatching of the heart."[22] To extend the metaphor, the heart is like an egg with a shell around it. If what is within is to live, the egg must hatch, the shell must break, the heart must open. If it does not, the life within dies and becomes foul-smelling and sulfuric.

The role of religion in the history of humankind is pervasively ambiguous. Although the spiritual function of religion is to aid the process of opening the heart and reorienting the self, religion can be used (and often has been used) as the ultimate legitimator of self-interest, whether by the group as a whole or by individuals. Groups have often justified their claims by grounding them in divine revelation, and individuals often legitimate their own positions by appeal to religious beliefs.[23] When this happens, religion can build an even thicker shell around the heart. But religion can also be the means of liberation from the self-interest of the encrusted heart into a wider community of being.

The spiritual journey, in Christian as well as non-Christian forms, is thus about the hatching of the heart, the opening of the self to the reality of the Spirit. This opening begins the process by which the self at its deepest level is reoriented and transformed.

How the Heart Is Opened

Sometimes it just happens. The process by which the heart is opened can be gradual or sudden. Some people seem more open to experiences of the Spirit, whether because of genetic disposition, personality type, or other reasons.[24] Sometimes the heart is broken open by experiences of grief or despair. Sometimes it comes "out of the blue" through a spontaneous religious experience or a dramatic conversion experience.[25] Sometimes it seems primarily to be the result of aging. There is nothing about aging that guarantees such a transformation (there are old people with hard hearts and bitter hearts), but aging, if not interfered with, does seem to have a softening effect. It is not coincidental that "wisdom" (meaning wisdom about living, not knowledge) is often associated with "the elders" (though, again, one can be an old fool). And sometimes it is the result of participation in the religious practices of a tradition.

Religious Practices and the Opening of the Heart

Many traditional religious practices have the effect of mediating the sacred and bringing about an opening of the heart. Some are collective in the double sense of typically being conducted in community and of being done because one is part of the community. Some are individual and intentional spiritual disciplines undertaken by persons seeking to be opened and nourished by a conscious relationship to the Spirit.[26]

In the broad sense of the word, all of these practices can be sacramental. Though the term *sacrament* can be used to refer to the specific sacraments of the church (seven in Catholic and Orthodox Christianity, two in most Protestant churches), its meaning in early Christianity was much broader. The Latin word *sacrament* translated the Greek word for "mystery" (meaning "sacred mystery") and referred to any spiritually symbolic object or practice that had a sacred character or function. A sacrament is a practice that makes the sacred mystery accessible. Its broad meaning is thus consistent with a common way of speaking about the specifically Christian sacraments: they are "means of grace," ways of mediating the sacred. As we survey traditional religious practices, we will focus on their sacramental function as incubators of the heart and mediators of the sacred.

COLLECTIVE PRACTICES

Because many ways of mediating the sacred are incorporated into the religious life of the group, they are experienced simply through participation in the group's religious life. Their transformative effects are often accidental: the person experiencing them may not be intending personal transformation or even aware that such might be the result. One experiences them because "this is what we do." A practicing Muslim prays five times a day, observes Ramadan (a month of fasting), and goes on pilgrimage to Mecca; a traditional Catholic goes regularly to mass, says the rosary, and makes the sign of the cross; an observant Orthodox Jew goes to synagogue, follows the laws of the Torah, and faithfully observes the Sabbath; and so forth. Observance can be by "rote" or "habit"—simply what one does if one takes a particular tradition seriously. But even when experienced because "this is what we do," these practices can have a profound spiritual effect on the heart.

The variety of ways used to mediate the sacred found within religious traditions is impressive. To illustrate this claim, I will briefly describe in quite general terms the spiritual functions of some common features of religious practice, highlighting the way in which they can mediate the sacred. Because I am most familiar with them, my examples will be drawn primarily from Jewish and Christian traditions.

Sacred Story. Hearing the sacred stories of the tradition in the context of worship can shape the imagination. The imagination is far more important in our lives than common modern associations with the term suggest; we tend to think of it as the realm of daydreams, fantasy, and (more positively) creativity. But it is more than that: it is the "home" of our images. Our imagination includes the collection of images and stories within our psyches that shape our sense of what is real, what life is about, and who we are. As such, the imagination is very powerful, profoundly affecting our sense of reality and identity.

Shaping and reshaping the imagination is one of the central functions of the public reading of Scripture as sacred story. These are the stories of our tribe, and they are also stories about God and us. As "our stories," they shape our sense of what it means to be part of this tradition (and not some other tradition). As stories about God and us, they shape our images of reality, of life, and of ourselves.

Though both the Jewish and Christian traditions contain other stories of central importance, one story is most central to each. For the Jewish tradition, it is the exodus story that includes slavery in Egypt, liberation from bondage, the giving of the Law at Sinai, the journey through the wilderness, and entry into the Promised Land. For the Christian tradition, it is of course the story of Jesus, understood as a single story and also as a collection of stories. Understood as stories about God and us, as disclosures of God and our identity in relationship to God, these stories can become internalized within our psyches and change the way we see our lives.[27]

Understood this way, Scripture as sacred story is not something to be believed in but a means for mediating the sacred. That is, Scripture is not to be treated as an object of belief but is to be lived within. It becomes a lens through which we "see" God, life, and ourselves and a means by which our imaginations are shaped by the sacred.

Sacred Rituals. Sacred story and sacred ritual are closely related. According to Mircea Eliade, probably our century's greatest historian of religions, sacred rituals are reenactments or embodiments of sacred story.[28] In the Jewish tradition, the exodus story is ritually reenacted in the celebration of Passover each year. In the Christian tradition, the two universal sacraments of baptism and Eucharist (or Lord's Supper, or mass) are both linked to Jesus. Ritualization enhances the power of the story. Through ritual, one relives the story. The elements of ritual function to create a sense of the sacred—of another reality. They commonly involve not only hearing but also seeing, singing, movement, sometimes even tasting and smelling. Like sacred story, but sometimes even more effectively, ritual can shape the religious imagination.

Sacred Time. Religions also use time as a way of mediating the sacred. One of the most familiar examples is the observance of the Sabbath in the Jewish tradition. The complete prohibition of work on the Sabbath creates one day a week unlike every other day: all work in or on the world stops. One day a week the world reverts to paradise, to the Garden of Eden, to the time before work began. Sabbath is not experienced as a day of inconvenient restrictions but as a day of joy. The most festive and sumptuous meal of the week welcomes the Sabbath. Husband and wife are expected to make love on the Sabbath, for they are Adam and Eve, the primal couple naked and unashamed in Eden, the Garden of Delight.

The Sabbath is one day a week of sacred time, of time out of time. It is a reminder of the reality of God and a taste of a paradise.[29]

Sacred Seasons. Time becomes sacramental in a somewhat different way in the liturgical seasons of the church year (Advent, Epiphany, Lent, Easter, Pentecost, and so forth). During each season one lives through a particular emphasis of the Christian life. Advent is a season of introspection in the midst of growing darkness as one simultaneously anticipates the coming of the light and the birth of Christ. Lent involves journeying with Jesus from Galilee to Jerusalem, following him on the path of discipleship, and participating in his death and resurrection. Liturgical seasons build the central dynamics of the Christian life into the rhythm of the year. Until the end of the Christian Middle Ages and the beginning of the modern period, ordinary people lived their lives in relationship to the liturgical seasons. The calendar itself functioned as a reminder and mediator of the sacred.

Sacred Sounds. Certain sounds seem to mediate the sacred. Here I am not speaking about music (which I will soon mention) or about the meaning of sounds (words) but about the sound of the sound itself. The use of extended open vowel sounds is common in religious traditions. A familiar example from Asian traditions is the syllable *om,* which is really a deep and prolonged *o* sound, with the final *m* simply being its protracted nasal continuation.[30] When spoken from deep within oneself, *om* resonates in a particular way. The same phenomenon is known in the Christian tradition. A similar effect is achieved by making the sounds, slowly and deeply, of *alleluia,* a common word of praise: ahh—lay—loo—yah.[31] The effectiveness of these sounds in creating an opening to the sacred can be intensified through repetitive chanting.

Sacred Music. Another use of sound comes in many forms, and it functions in different ways. Some sacred music (choral or instrumental) is performed for the worshiping congregation, and some is participatory, sung or chanted by the worshipers themselves. Performed music can mediate the sacred through the experience of beauty or by creating a sense of another reality. Participatory music can also do so, but it has further functions. Through it, one becomes part of a community and harmony of sacred sound. Moreover, the opportunity to "sing one's heart out" is provided by accessible hymns that can be sung with enthusiasm.[32] In hymns of praise, we often experience being drawn out of ourselves.

Indeed, for many Protestants, such hymn singing is the primary way the heart is softened and opened.

Sacred Speech. By "sacred speech," I mean ecstatic religious utterance. I do not mean the reading of Scripture or the preaching of sermons. Known in many religious traditions, ecstatic religious utterance in the Christian tradition is commonly called "speaking in tongues," or glossolalia. Though it can be done privately, it is also part of the collective worship experience of Pentecostal Christians. Often misunderstood by people unfamiliar with it, it is typically not experienced as an involuntary seizure or compulsion over which one has no control but as the Spirit praying (or singing) through one. It is involuntary ("nonthinking") in the sense that one does not decide what to say, but otherwise it can be entered into. The nonlanguage language of the Spirit becomes the vehicle for mediating the Spirit.

Sacred Silence. The absence of sound has also been a sacrament of the sacred. In groups gathered for worship, silence can be used either as one element in the service or as the primary element, as in the Quaker tradition. In some monastic orders, silence is a way of life (except for liturgical speaking). Silence may be understood as the appropriate response to the presence of the sacred, or as waiting and listening for the Spirit, or as the experience of communion with the Spirit.[33] By stopping the flow of words and sounds, silence invites us into a wordless world. It also conveys the sense that something is present that is worth attending to.

Sacred Images. Sacred art in general can open the heart to the sacred. Paintings, stained glass windows, and sculpture remind worshipers of specific biblical characters and stories and the lives of the saints. But the sacramental role of sacred images is perhaps best seen in the use of icons (from the Greek word for image) in the Orthodox Christian tradition. Icons are highly stylized paintings of a sacred subject. Their purpose is not to display the creativity or virtuosity of an individual artist but to point to the sacred. Indeed, they do more than point; intended to be used in meditative prayer, their purpose is to become windows to the sacred through which we "see" God and God "sees" us. They mediate the sacred by becoming transparent to that which is beyond, thereby making the beyond present.[34]

Sacred Space. Space is also used to mediate a sense of the sacred. Worship space—both the architecture of the space and the ambiance of the space—commonly functions to mediate a sense of another world. Orthodox churches provide a particularly good example. The internal space of the church building and what happens there—from the use of subdued light, holy icons, and elaborate vestments to the smoke and smell of incense and the sung liturgy—create a sense that we are temporarily entering another world. The words over the door of the church confirm the impression: the kingdom of God. When one enters this space, one enters a different reality.

Sacred Journey. Pilgrimage is a journey to a sacred place. In ancient Israel, pilgrimage was to Jerusalem, the city of God where God dwelt in the temple. Groups of pilgrims commonly traveled together, and there is even a collection of psalms that were used as they "went up" to Jerusalem.[35] In Christianity, pilgrimage has been to many places: Jerusalem, Rome, Canterbury, and other pilgrimage sites in Europe and Latin America. Symbolically, pilgrimage is a sacred journey: a journeying toward God. It expresses the yearning of the heart to be in the presence of God; because during pilgrimage the self is pointed toward its destination, it is a physical embodiment of inclining the heart toward God.

Sacred Laws. Perhaps the most familiar example of detailed observance of God's laws as a way of shaping the heart is Orthodox Judaism.[36] Orthodox Jews are committed to observing the whole of the Torah, both the written Torah of 613 commandments and the greatly expanded and highly detailed oral Torah (as codified in the Mishnah and Talmud). The laws pertain to virtually every aspect of life: daily prayers, what to eat, how to cut your hair, blessings and thanksgivings for everything from eating to relieving oneself, and so forth. Christians (especially Protestants) have not had much sympathy for or understanding of this way of being religious. Usually dismissed as "life under the law," it is seen as the life of requirements in contrast to the life of faith and grace. But this easy dismissal ignores the fact that this way of being religious has not only nourished the lives of ordinary people through the centuries but also produced many saints and mystics.

Though an emphasis on observing God's laws can lead to self-righteousness and judgmentalism ("we the good people" follow God's law, while others don't—an attitude found in both Jewish and Christian forms), the emphasis can also have a quite different effect. Namely, it can incline the heart toward God. Observing God's laws in the myriad details of the everyday provides a constant reminder of the reality of God and shapes the self in the direction of God. Through the practice of hallowing the everyday, the heart can become centered in God.

Sacred Worship. Many of the features just described are part of sacred worship. As with observance of the law, one may go to worship services out of habit or because it is "what we do." But what happens during worship can function to mediate the Spirit. Church services do this in various ways. Some are charismatic, in which the gifts of the Spirit are manifestly present in the community; some create a sense of another reality through sacrament and liturgy; some use silence as a way of being in the presence of God; some depend primarily on music (including the enthusiastic singing of hymns) as a way of opening the heart; some emphasize the spoken word of Scripture and preaching. These emphases can, of course, be combined.

When worship is functioning as it should, it can be a powerful mediator of the sacred. It can open the heart, shape the religious imagination, and nourish the spiritual life, all within the experience of community. Unfortunately, worship does not always work this way. It can be dead and dispirited. Modern noncharismatic Protestant Christianity seems particularly vulnerable to this. To a large extent, Protestant churches have abandoned many of the traditional mediators of the sacred: the use of sacred time, space, sound, silence, images, journey, and even rituals is often underdeveloped and poorly understood.

There is more than one reason for this loss. Protestantism began as a protest against late medieval Catholicism; the rejection of Catholic tradition meant also the rejection of many of these practices. Protestantism has also been most open to the Enlightenment and the development of industrial society. Practices that did not make sense within an Enlightenment worldview were abandoned as superstitious. Worship services were streamlined to make "efficient" use of time (mainline Protestant services that last more than an hour typically become the subject of complaints).

The result is that the spoken word has come to dominate many Protestant forms of worship: the words of prayers, responsive readings, Scripture, the sermon, and so forth. Yet the spoken word is perhaps the least effective way of reaching the heart; one must constantly pay attention with one's mind. The spoken word tends to go to our heads, not our hearts. This dependence on the spoken word can be compensated for by the other central feature of much Protestant worship: the singing of hymns. When these are well chosen (ones that can be sung from the heart), the service can still "work" as a sacrament of the sacred. But if dependence on the spoken word is combined with hymns that are difficult to sing, the service does not function well as a mediator of the sacred. Granted, the Spirit can work anywhere and through anything—but there seems to be little point in making the Spirit's work more difficult.

Moreover, a congregation whose worship service is not experienced as a mediator of the sacred is unlikely to survive very long. To recall an earlier comment, churches that are full of God are likely to find their pews full of people.

The present impoverishment of some forms of Protestant worship does not need to persist. The Christian tradition's rich memory of practices that mediate the sacred remains and can be reclaimed. The spiritual wisdom of the past is a resource for our time and can be brought into the present, adapted as necessary. What is needed is a sensitivity to the Spirit and not simply a sensitivity to the spirit of the age.

Almost a century ago, William James distinguished between secondhand religion and firsthand religious experience.[37] Secondhand religion is what we learn from others; it includes everything we learn from tradition. Firsthand religious experience is our own experience of the sacred. All of the practices I have described are thus part of secondhand religion. Yet their spiritual function is to mediate firsthand religious experience: to bring about an opening of the heart to the reality of the sacred all around us.

INDIVIDUAL PRACTICES

In addition to these collective means, religious traditions have also developed a variety of practices for individuals. Commonly called spiritual disciplines, they offer ways of becoming more intentional about the hatching of the heart and life with God. Of these, two are most important: prayer and deeds of compassion.

Prayer. Prayer, of course, is also part of collective worship life, which typically includes prayers spoken by the worship leaders as well as by the congregation. But here I focus on the spiritual functions of prayer as practiced by individuals outside of public worship settings. In the Christian tradition (as in most traditions), such prayer includes both verbal and nonverbal forms. Verbal prayer includes both those spoken out loud and those said silently; nonverbal prayer includes various forms of meditation and contemplation.[38]

When I was a child, I only knew about verbal prayer. Though our worship services included "a moment of silent prayer," these moments were very brief, and I assumed that during them we each were to offer up our own verbal prayers. Moreover, as a child I thought of prayer primarily as asking God for something (I have since learned to call this "petitionary" prayer). Of course, there were prayers of thanksgiving as well, but even these were often petitionary. Our table graces asked Jesus to be present. At home before meals, we prayed, "Come, Lord Jesus, be our guest, and let these gifts to us be blessed." At special meals, we used a longer prayer that was also petitionary: "Be present at our table, Lord; be here and everywhere adored; these mercies bless, and grant that we may feast in paradise with thee." At bedtime, I petitioned God for protection: "Now I lay me down to sleep, I pray the Lord my soul to keep; if I should die before I wake, I pray the Lord my soul to take." This was followed by asking God to bless those whom I loved (Mom and Dad, brothers and sisters, uncles and aunts, cousins, friends), as well as persons unknown to me ("all the sick people").

These were prayers I had been taught; I knew them by rote. But I also prayed on my own. Again, asking God for something was dominant. Sometimes I asked God for help, for myself or for others, in particular situations. Sometimes I asked for things. Sometimes I prayed for forgiveness. Behind all of this was the notion of God described earlier in this book: the supernatural interventionist model. I took it for granted that God was a being "out there" who could answer any prayer God wanted to and that God decided to answer some prayers but not others. A friend once called this an image of God as a cosmic bellhop (though apparently a bellhop with an independent streak).

But the way of seeing God sketched in this book significantly changes how we see prayer. Seeing God as "the one in whom we live and move and have our being" means that prayer is not addressing a distant being who may or may not be there and who may or may not answer. Rather, within the framework of seeing God as "right here" and "all around us," as one with whom we are already in relationship whether we know it or not, prayer (verbal and nonverbal) becomes the primary individual means of consciously entering into and nurturing a relationship with God. Prayer is attending to our relationship with God.[39]

Verbal prayer addresses God with words. Whether practiced out loud, silently, or by journaling, its central quality is that it is said to God as

"You," as the presence who is right here. Thus it is conversational: it is simply talking to God. And not (if one takes nonmonarchical images of God seriously) as one would talk to a king or authoritarian father but as one would talk to a lover, friend, spouse, intimate parent. In such relationships, we simply talk about whatever is on our mind: how we're feeling, what we're dealing with in our lives, what's happened in our day, and so on. In such relationships, we also listen; ideally, conversational prayer will include listening as well as talking.

Conversational prayer often involves asking for something, as the prayers of my childhood did. I sometimes ask for something for myself: energy, or presence, or clarity. I sometimes ask for something for somebody else, usually protection or healing. I have no idea how petitionary and intercessory prayer works. I cannot explain it with an interventionist model of God, for to do so implies that God decides to respond to some requests but not others. I cannot reconcile such a notion of God with collective brutalities such as the Holocaust and the often arbitrary character of private tragedy. I cannot believe that God could have stopped the Holocaust but chose not to, just as I cannot believe that God responds to some prayers for healing and protection but not others. Yet I am also convinced that paranormal things happen, even though I can't imagine an explanation. And so, though I don't think of God as an interventionist, I still make requests of God. It seems to be a natural part of the relationship to do so, just as it feels like a way of caring for people.

What is the function of verbal conversational prayer, of simply talking to God? How does it work as a means of opening and reorienting the self? It has a number of subtle effects that become cumulative. Doing so "reminds" one of God. Much as the detailed observance of sacred laws in the midst of the ordinary reminds Orthodox Jews of the reality of God, daily prayer does the same thing. Moreover, the sheer act of doing it (regardless of content) takes seriously that life is a relationship with God: that God is there to be addressed (and to be addressed by), that the sacred is a "You" and not an "it." Conversational prayer acts on and embodies this notion. Such prayer is also a way of "spending time" in the relationship. The analogy to close human relationships is instructive: relationships are nurtured by spending time in them.

In my own case, I know that when I remember to talk to God, my life generally goes better. My own practice is to talk out loud, commonly in my car (which somebody has referred to as the modern equivalent of a monastic cell). On days I remember to do so, I usually feel more centered, more present, more open, more peaceful, and more appreciative. Yet I can so easily forget. When I go three or four days without "remembering" God (even though I might be thinking about God a lot, as when writing this book), my life has the opposite qualities: less centered, less present, less open, less peaceful, less appreciative. How I can know this and yet sometimes forget to pray remains a puzzle to me.

Much of what I have said about verbal prayer also applies to *nonverbal prayer:* it reminds one of God; it takes seriously that God is here; it is attending to and spending time in the relationship. But nonverbal prayer works in a different way. It has many forms. Some forms use images from Scripture; some employ a mantra (a word or short phrase used repetitively); some involve sitting silently and watching whatever arises in one's mind without becoming involved with it; some involve focusing on one's breath.

In general, its many forms have in common stilling the mind before God. Doing so is not as easy as it might sound. I sometimes involve my students in a "stop thinking for one minute" exercise. I explain that I want them to turn off the internal flow of words for one minute, then lead them into a meditative state; afterward I poll them on how they've done. Most often, only one or two out of fifty report being able to turn off the words. If we had as little control over our bodies as we seem to have over our minds, we would have difficulty walking. The mind is busy, noisy, distracting. Nonverbal prayer involves learning how to become silent inside.

I first learned about nonverbal prayer as a part of other religious traditions. I did not know that it also has a long history in the Christian tradition (even though I had gone to a first-rate seminary; I do not know if it was not taught or if I missed it). It intrigued me. I learned about the use of mantras as a means of giving the mind something to focus and refocus on as it sinks into silence. I was thus delighted to learn later that the Christian tradition not only knows the practice of nonverbal prayer but also includes mantras. One of the most famous is the rosary; though saying the rosary can be done out of habit or for penance, the effect of the multiple repetitions is like that of a mantra. Another famous Christian mantra is the Jesus Prayer of the Orthodox tradition: "Lord Jesus Christ, Son of God, have mercy." I used it for many years until I was taught a modified form whose words I like better: "Lord Jesus Christ, you are the light of the world; fill my mind with your peace, and my heart with your love." I use it both as a mantra and as a brief centering prayer.

In practice, verbal and nonverbal prayer are often combined. Many people who have a regular prayer time of thirty minutes may spend the first five or ten minutes in verbal or conversational prayer (perhaps including thanksgiving, introspection, petitions and intercessions, and so forth) and then move into a form of nonverbal prayer.

The internal silence of nonverbal prayer can function in a number of ways. When used with images, it creates space for God to speak to us through the imagination. Or it can lead to the state of acquired contemplation (actually becoming silent inside) that sometimes moves into infused contemplation (the experience of God's presence in the silence of wordlessness). To use an image I owe to Alan Jones, nonverbal prayer involves the attentiveness of a bird-watcher: as one watches silently and motionlessly, the forest can become alive.

The cumulative effect of praying to God as the "You" in our midst, whether verbally or nonverbally, is that one's sense of God, life, and oneself begins to change. Prayer transforms those who pray.

Deeds of Compassion. A quite different path leading to the opening of the heart is compassion. Because I am about to speak of compassion as a means of internal transformation, I want to begin by emphasizing that deeds of compassion are important in their own right in the Christian tradition. Compassion is not just a means of spiritual transformation but an end in itself. It is the central ethical value of the Jesus tradition, as well as the central quality of God. Moreover, it also has political meaning, which I will develop in the next chapter.

But compassion is also a movement within the self, and this is the aspect I want to highlight now. In the Bible, there is a feeling dimension to compassion: people are moved by compassion, a feeling felt deep within oneself. For women, compassion is felt in the womb (to which the word is related in Hebrew); for men, in the bowels. Compassion means to be moved within oneself as a mother is moved by tenderness and concern for the children of her womb. The roots of the English word suggest the same family of meaning: compassion means "to feel with" and thus to feel the feelings and situation of another.[40] It is especially associated with feeling the suffering of others.

Compassion is thus being moved in one's heart, at a level of the self below the mind. It begins with presence, for it flows out of being present to the plight of others. Of course, it does not automatically do so; one can "harden one's heart" in the presence of suffering. But being present to the plight of others can soften the heart.

Sometimes situations come along in our lives that give birth to compassion. But one can also be more deliberate. Intentionally placing oneself in situations where people are struggling and need help, and being present to that experience, can be transformative. For people like me and many of the readers of this book whose life circumstances are reasonably secure, there are a variety of ways of doing this: serving a meal once a week or month in a soup kitchen, working as a volunteer in any number of agencies, building a house with Habitat for Humanity, and so on. Compassion can even be birthed by being really present to the evening news, though I am not suggesting watching television as a primary means. What matters for this means of transformation is letting the life circumstances of others move one's heart.[41]

Some people find the experience and practice of compassion as a spiritual discipline to be a more direct route to the transformation of the heart than prayer. It is not that prayer does not or should not play a role in their lives, but their way to the opening of the heart lies through deeds of compassion. "Just do it" summarizes this path of transformation.

In addition to prayer and deeds of compassion, there are other individual practices that can nurture the opening of the self to the sacred and its reorientation to life with God. These include dream work, nature or wilderness experiences, solitude, fasting, silence for extended periods of time (alone or with a group), spiritual retreats (again, alone or with a group), spiritual reading, and working with a spiritual director or spiritual friend.[42]

Personality Types and the Opening of the Heart

What practice or combination of practices will work best varies from individual to individual. Some of this variation is because we are each different; and some may be related to personality type. Huston Smith's exposition of the four *yogas,* or paths of spiritual transformation, in traditional Hinduism makes the point well.[43] Related to the English word *yoke, yoga* has the double connotation of uniting together (being yoked) and undertaking training (as in "Take my yoke upon you"). A *yoga* is thus a path of reunion: a practical means of reconnecting with the sacred in a conscious way.

The four *yogas* correspond to four basic spirituality types: reflective (thinking), emotional (feeling), active (doing), and contemplative (experiencing). In the same order, *jnana yoga* (with the *j* pronounced as a *g*) is the way of the intellect, in which one's mind is directed toward God. *Bhakti yoga* is the path of devotion and adoration, in which one's love is directed toward God. *Karma yoga* is the path of deeds, in which one's work and actions are directed toward God. *Raja yoga* emphasizes spiritual and physical exercises as a way of opening the heart and directing the whole of the self toward God.

For many people, depending on personality type, one of these paths is likely to be primary, even though elements from one or more of the other paths are likely to be integrated as well. Prayer, for example, is likely to be part of all four paths—though what type of prayer, as well as its proportional place in the spiritual life, will vary.[44]

What works best needs to be discovered by each person.

SPIRITUALITY AND TRANSFORMATION

Spirituality is thus for the hatching of the heart. Whatever helps to open our hearts to the reality of the sacred is what we should be engaged in. This awareness leads to an image of the Christian life very different from the one with which I grew up. The Christian life is not about pleasing God the finger-shaker and judge. It is not about believing now or being good now for the sake of heaven later. It is about entering a relationship in the present that begins to change everything now. Spirituality is about this process: the opening of the heart to the God who is already here.

The fruit of this process is compassion. As mentioned earlier, compassion is not simply a means for the self's transformation but also the end or goal of such transformation. God's will for us—the goal of the working of the Spirit within us—is to become more compassionate beings. Such was Saint Paul's point when he spoke of the greatest of the spiritual gifts as love, his more abstract term for what Jesus meant by compassion. If spirituality—a life of relationship with the Spirit of God—does not lead to compassion, then either it is life in relationship to a different spirit or there is a lot of static in the relationship. The absence or presence of compassion is the central test for discerning whether something is "of God." As the primary gift of the Spirit, compassion is the primary sign of spiritual growth.

The Christian life as life in the Spirit thus involves a process of transformation quickened within us by the Spirit of God. It is expressed with exquisite elegance by Saint Paul, in one of those passages that virtually glows:

> And we all, with unveiled faces, beholding the glory of the Lord Christ, are being changed into his likeness from one degree of glory to another; and this comes from the Lord who is the Spirit.[45]

Notes

1. I owe the phrase to Frederick J. Streng, *Understanding Religious Life,* second ed., (Encino, CA: Dickenson, 1976), p. 7.

2. Gen. 3.24.

3. A phrase that I owe to John Hick. See his *Evil and the God of Love* (London: Macmillan, 1966), p. 317–27.

4. Loren Eiseley, *The Invisible Pyramid* (New York: Charles Scribner's Sons, 1970), pp. 119–20.

5. Rom. 1.25: we "worship and serve the creature rather than the Creator."

6. For Buber's notion of I-It and I-You, see Chapter Two in this book.

7. Paul Tillich, *Theology of Culture,* ed. Robert Kimball (New York: Oxford University Press, 1959), p. 43.

8. We will be concerned with several in the concluding chapter.

9. Examples: hard heart: Ps. 95.8; Prov. 28.14; Isa. 63.17; Mark 3.5, 6.52, 8.17, 10.5; John 12.40; Acts 28.27; Heb. 3.8, 15; 4.7. Heart of stone: Ezek. 11.19, 36.26. Closed and shut: Isa. 44.18. Fat heart: Isa. 6.10. Proud heart: Isa. 9.9, Prov. 21.4, 28.25; Hos. 13.6. Modern translations (such as the RSV and NRSV) sometimes obscure the presence of "heart" in the text by translating the Hebrew word with "mind." This translation does make the point, however, that the heart is associated with thought in ancient Hebrew psychology.

10. In sequence: Job 23.16; 2 Kings 22.19; Ezek. 11.19, 36.26; Ps. 51.17.

11. Isa. 6.10. The RSV and NRSV translate "make the *heart* of this people fat" with "make the *mind* of this people dull."

12. Mark 8.17.

13. Isa. 44.18. Again the RSV and NRSV translate "heart" with "mind" in this verse.

14. In sequence: Isa. 9.9; Prov. 28.25, 21.4; Hos. 13.6.

15. Isa. 63.17.

16. Mark 3.5.

17. Ps. 95.7b–11.

18. Ezek. 11.19, 36.26.

19. Ps. 51.10.

20. Jer. 31.31–34.

21. Because of a Christian tendency to identify the old covenant with the Hebrew Bible and Judaism and the new covenant with the New Testament and Christianity, I emphasize that "old covenant" and "new covenant" are *ways of being* known in both Judaism and Christianity. There are "old covenant" ways of being Christian, just as there are "new covenant" ways of being Jewish.

22. I owe the phrase to one of Alan Jones's very helpful books, *Exploring Spiritual Direction* (New York: Seabury, 1982), whose epilogue is titled "For the Hatching of the Heart" (pp. 127–30). Jones cites the use of the image in Frederick Buechner's novel *Godric* (New York: Atheneum, 1980).

23. Langdon Gilkey's *Shantung Compound* (New York: Harper & Row, 1966) is a fascinating account of the ambiguous relationship between self-interest and religious beliefs (including beliefs about God), flowing out of his experience in a civilian internment camp in China during World War II. As Gilkey points out, the process of legitimating self-interest is often unconscious; the group or individual is not aware that he or she is rationalizing self-interest by appealing to the will of God. Gilkey's experience led him to a revisioning of Christian understandings of sin, faith, and salvation.

24. See William James's remark about persons who seem to be born with a couple of bottles of champagne to their credit; *Varieties of Religious Experience,* p. 135.

25. One of the most famous of these is Saint Paul's "Damascus Road" experience (see Chapter Four in this book). In one sense, the experience was spontaneous and unexpected, yet one must also remember that Paul had embarked on a very serious and intense religious journey long before the experience happened (he was, after all, sufficiently zealous and devout that he was persecuting a group for religious reasons). One of the most extended and interesting descriptions of the psychological process of sudden conversion experiences remains William James, *Varieties of Religious Experience,* Chapter Ten.

26. I do not know the scholarly literature in these areas as well as I do in the other areas treated in this book. What follows flows out of a general awareness of the purpose and function of religious practices.

27. For a compact introduction to "story theology" and what I call the three "macrostories" of Scripture, see Chapter Six of my *Meeting Jesus Again for the First Time.*

28. Eliade, *The Sacred and the Profane,* and *Myth and Reality* (New York: Harper & Row, 1963).

29. In modern Christianity (and in the modern Western world generally), we have lost a sense of sacred time. Time has been homogenized. Though the majority of people have the weekend "off," it is typically filled with ordinary busy-ness: catching up on work and household chores, buying and selling, recreational activities, and so forth. In the name of freedom, work has penetrated every moment of the week. A very helpful book on reclaiming the Sabbath for Christians is Tilden Edwards's *Sabbath Time* (Nashville, TN: Upper Room, 1992).

30. See Rudolf Otto's interesting appendix on "Original Numinous Sounds" in his *The Idea of the Holy,* pp. 190–93. Otto focuses on the origin of these sounds (he refers to "the long-protracted vowel of wonder," p. 191), whereas I am focusing more on their function. See also Tilden Edwards, *Living in the Presence* (San Francisco: Harper & Row, 1987), pp. 34–43.

31. Other examples of Hebrew and Aramaic words with extended open vowel sounds that function in a similar way: Adonai (one of the names of God); Yeshuah (Jesus in Aramaic); *abba* (father) and *amma* (mother).

32. The roots of the word *enthusiasm* mean "in God."

33. See another appendix, "Silent Worship," in Otto, *The Idea of the Holy,* pp. 210–14.

34. For a brief introduction to icons and their sacramental use, see Edwards, *Living in the Presence,* pp. 45–53.

35. Pss. 120–34, known as "the psalms of ascent." Because Jerusalem is on a high ridge, one needs to "ascend" to get to Jerusalem from whatever direction one is traveling.

36. A similar emphasis is found in some Christian sectarian movements. However, Christians for the most part have radically simplified the laws of God into a short list.

37. James, *Varieties of Religious Experience,* lecture one.

38. "Meditation" and "contemplation" are often used interchangeably as umbrella terms for all forms of nonverbal prayer. Some authors argue that they are quite different and should be carefully distinguished; see, for example, Tilden Edwards, *Living in the Presence,* n. 2, pp. 159–60.

39. Though I have done some reading in this area, I am not widely read in this rapidly growing field; though I follow some spiritual practices, I am not as experienced as many. Thus what I have to say in this section is how I see things, given these limitations. Among books with which I am familiar, I recommend the following: in the category of "how to" books, Marjorie J. Thompson's *Soul Feast: An Invitation to the Christian Spiritual Life* (Louisville, KY: Westminster John Knox, 1995) is a fine introduction to a variety of practices, with extensive annotated bibliography; Edwards's *Living in the Presence* is another fine introduction to individual and group practices; Richard Foster, in *Prayer: Finding the Heart's True Home* (San Francisco: HarperSanFrancisco, 1992), introduces twenty different kinds of prayer; Flora Slosson Wuellner, in *Prayer and Our Bodies* (Nashville, TN: Upper Room, 1987), emphasizes praying for and with our bodies (Wuellner's other books are also recommended); Anthony Bloom, *Beginning to Pray* (New York: Paulist, 1970); Martin L. Smith, *The Word Is Very Near You: A Guide to Praying with Scripture* (Cambridge, MA: Cowley, 1989). The following are more *about* prayer, though they contain practical guidance as well: William Shannon, *Seeking the Face of God* (New York: Crossroad, 1992); Henri Nouwen, *The Way of the Heart* (San Francisco: Harper & Row, 1981)—Nouwen is generally excellent for spiritual reading; Kenneth Leech, in *True Prayer: An Invitation to Christian Spirituality* (San Francisco: HarperSanFrancisco, 1986) and *The Eye of the Storm: Living Spiritually in the Real World* (San Francisco: HarperSanFrancisco, 1992), emphasizes the connection between spirituality and social justice; Roberta Bondi, *To Pray and to Love* (Minneapolis: Augsburg-Fortress, 1991), and *In Ordinary Time*.

40. Compassion is not to be confused with codependency, which means feeling the feelings of others to such an extent that one has no center of one's own.

41. Of course, one can *act* compassionately even from a distance (with money or by voting, to mention two examples), but the *experience* of compassion involves presence.

42. For dream work in a Christian context, see especially Morton Kelsey, *God, Dreams, and Revelations,* rev. ed. (Minneapolis: Augsburg, 1991); John A. Sanford, *Dreams and Healing* (New York: Paulist, 1978). For a personal and insightful introduction to spiritual retreats, spiritual direction, spiritual reading, small groups, and even spirituality "on-line," see Debra Farrington, *Romancing the Holy* (New York: Crossroad, 1997). See also Thompson, *Soul Feast,* and Edwards, *Sabbath Time* and *Living in the Presence.*

43. Smith, *The World's Religions* (San Francisco: HarperSanFrancisco, 1991), pp. 26–50. Smith's compact yet nicely detailed exposition of the four *yogas* strikes me as beautiful, insightful, and inspiring.

44. Smith, *The World's Religions*, p. 28, notes that Carl Jung's theory of personality types is indebted to Hinduism's four yogas. Chester P. Michael and Marie C. Norrisey, in *Prayer and Temperament: Different Prayer Forms for Different Personality Types* (Charlottesville, VA: Open Door, 1991), correlate spirituality with Jungian (Myers-Briggs) personality types.

45. 2 Cor. 3.18. It is interesting that Paul can use Lord, Christ, and Spirit interchangeably.

CHAPTER 6

THE DREAM
OF GOD:

A POLITICS OF
COMPASSION

Seek justice, and live.[1]

Contemporary social etiquette advises, "Avoid talking about religion or politics." In this chapter, we will talk about both. They are more closely related than we often imagine. Just as how we think about God affects our thinking about nature, gender, Jesus, spirituality, and the internal dynamic of the Christian life, it also affects our political thinking.

Some ways of thinking about God legitimate the existing political order, claiming that kings rule by "divine right" or by "the grace of God" and that the powers that be are ordained by God.[2] Obedience to God the heavenly king requires obedience to the earthly king as well. The result is a social order identified as "God's will."

Other ways of thinking about God do not explicitly legitimate the political order but leave it undisturbed by treating it as irrelevant to the religious life. This happens when Christianity (or religion generally) is seen as primarily concerned with the individual's relationship with God, whether the stakes are life after death or peace of mind in this life. "Where will you spend eternity?" tends to shift one's focus away from this world and render political questions of little importance. So also do forms of spirituality (Christian and post-Christian) that stress primarily the self and its fulfillment.[3] Life is separated into two spheres: a private realm of religion and a public realm of economics and politics.[4] Commitments in one realm are kept separate from commitments in the other.

And some ways of thinking about God lead to a passion for a transformed social order. In our own century, we have seen this in figures like Mahatma Gandhi, Dorothy Day, Martin Luther King Jr., and Desmond Tutu and in movements such as liberation theology and Latin-American Christian "base communities." The conviction that God cares about suffering leads to protest against unjust social orders and advocacy of an alternative social vision.

These different ways of thinking about the connection between the sacred and the world of politics account for the profoundly ambiguous relationship between religion and culture in human history. Religion sometimes functions as the ultimate world-domesticating force by declaring that the order and structure of culture reflect the will of God—and sometimes as the ultimate world-subverting force by proclaiming that God wills otherwise.

Both visions of God and the social order are found in the Bible itself. Indeed, the opposition between these two visions is a central tension running throughout the biblical tradition, from the birth of ancient Israel to the book of Revelation. Vision of God and social vision go together.

THE DREAM OF GOD

One of these visions is "the dream of God." I owe the phrase to the title of a recent book by Verna Dozier.⁵ In a broad sense, the Bible as a whole is the story of the dream of God, beginning in Genesis with paradise and ending with paradise restored in the great concluding vision of the book of Revelation. The first paradise is two individuals in a garden, and the second paradise is communal and urban—the new Jerusalem, the city of God.

Yet the dream of God is not the whole of the biblical story, for the Bible also includes the nightmarish elements introduced by what happens in human history. The Bible speaks about the rejection of the dream as well as the dream itself. Thus, in a narrower sense, the dream of God is a social and political vision of a world of justice and peace in which human beings do not hurt or destroy, oppress or exploit one another. It is the dream expressed with many images and by many voices in the Bible:

They will all sit under their own vines and under their own fig trees,
    and no one shall make them afraid.[6]

They will beat their swords into plowshares,
and their spears into pruning hooks;
nation shall not lift up sword against nation,
neither shall they learn war anymore.[7]

The mountains shall drip sweet wine, and all the hills shall flow with it.[8]

The dream of God is a vision of *shalom,* a rich Hebrew word often translated as "peace" but meaning much more than the absence of war. It means well-being in a comprehensive sense. It includes freedom from negatives such as oppression, anxiety, and fear, as well as the presence of positives such as health, prosperity, and security. *Shalom* thus includes a social vision: the dream of a world in which such well-being belongs to everybody.

As the story of the interaction between the dream of God and the rejection of the dream through what happens in history, the Bible is a tale of two kingdoms: the kingdom of God and the kingdoms of this world.

THE SOCIAL WORLD OF THE BIBLE

In order to see the tension between these two kingdoms, these two ways of being and living in community, we begin with a picture of the most common type of society (including social, economic, and political dimensions) in the world in which ancient Israel and the Bible came into existence.

This was the social world of the "preindustrial agrarian society," sometimes abbreviated as "peasant society."[9] This type of society is easiest to envision when we place it within the sequence of human social development. Preindustrial agrarian societies began about six thousand years ago. They were preceded by simple horticultural societies in which agricultural production (using digging sticks and hoes) was modest, and only small concentrations of population (at the most, villages and towns) could be supported in one place. Preindustrial agrarian societies emerged when agriculture became sufficiently productive (through the use of the plow) to generate surpluses that could support larger concentrations of population. In short, cities were born.

Preindustrial cities were small by modern standards. On average, 10 percent of the population lived in cities, while the other 90 percent remained rural. The rural population was made up primarily of agricultural producers (peasants, from which we get "peasant society").[10] In such societies, agriculture was the primary source of wealth. There was as yet no industry; manufacturing was by hand and small scale. This type of society lasted in various forms until the beginning of the industrial revolution, and it persists in some developing parts of the world to this day.

Of greatest importance for our purpose is the social structure of preindustrial agrarian societies. The division between city and country corresponded with a class division of power and wealth between urban elites and rural peasants. The urban elites consisted of two groups. First there were the elites proper, typically 1 to 2 percent of the total population: the ruler, aristocrats, high government and religious officials, and their extended families. Second, attached to the elites was a service class known as retainers, typically 5 to 8 percent of the population: lower-ranking government officials, soldiers, priests, scribes, urban merchants, and so forth.

The economic gulf between urban elites and rural peasants was enormous. Elites and their retainers (together, less than 10 percent of the population) acquired about two-thirds of the society's annual production of wealth, with about half of the total going to the top 1 to 2 percent. Rural peasants (90 percent of the population) made do with the remaining one-third.[11]

How did the urban elites manage to do this? They didn't produce anything. They provided few services (going to war being one of their chief ones). Rather, they got their wealth from the only source of wealth there was: the agricultural production of peasants. The elites used two primary means of extracting wealth: taxation of peasant production and ownership of agricultural land (which could then be rented by peasants, or farmed through the use of laborers or slaves). Elites were very good at calculating exactly how much they could take without driving peasants into starvation or resistance. This is not surprising, for their wealth depended on this relationship of economic exploitation. Moreover, wars were often fought between elites in order to acquire control over more peasants; this was the only way in which their wealth could be increased. The cumulative effect on peasants was dreadful. Peasant existence was vulnerable to subsistence diet, drought, illness, war, even the death of an animal. Life expectancy was very low.[12]

In these societies, religion most often functioned to legitimate the social order: God had ordained that it be this way. At least the religion of the elites did, as it has come down to us through their retainers of priests and scribes. For the most part, we do not have access to the religion of peasants, who left few or no written records.

Thus "peasant society" was the dominant type of social organization in the world in which the Bible came into existence. City-states and eventually agrarian empires emerged in Egypt and Mesopotamia beginning around 4000 B.C.E. By the time of ancient Israel's origin, this type of society was firmly entrenched in the ancient Middle East. Ruled by elites, such societies were intrinsically hierarchical, economically exploitative, and politically oppressive.

THE EXODUS AND THE DREAM OF GOD

The dream of God is expressed paradigmatically in Israel's foundational narrative, the story of the exodus from Egypt. The most important story ancient Israel knew, the exodus story was told and retold in sacred writings, celebrated in hymns, and relived annually in the festival of Passover. It was not only the story of Israel's origins but also a story about God. As an epiphany of God's involvement in her history and life, it disclosed both the character and will of God.

Strikingly, Israel's foundational narrative was a story of liberation from the domination system of a peasant society.[13] The Egypt in which her ancestors had become slaves was a classic agrarian empire. As Walter Brueggemann puts it, the lordship of Pharaoh reflected "royal consciousness," a way of seeing and organizing life from the vantage point of the elites. Egypt was marked by an economics of exploitation, a politics of oppression, and a religion of legitimation.[14]

According to Israel's story of the exodus, however, God was not impressed with the glories of the royal court but rather was moved by the suffering of the Hebrew slaves and willed their freedom. God heard their groans:

> The Israelites groaned under their slavery, and cried. Out of the slavery their cry for help rose up to God, and God heard their groaning.[15]

God felt their misery:"I know their sufferings."[16] Moved to act, God liberated them from Egypt through the leadership of Moses, entered into a covenant with them at Sinai, and brought them to the Promised Land.

There, in accord with their understanding of God's will, they sought to create a domination-free social order radically different from that of Egypt. For the first couple of centuries, the Hebrew tribes had no centralized government and thus no monarchy and no elites. Instead, God was king. Moreover, every family was allocated a portion of land, to be theirs in perpetuity.[17] The lack of centralization and the guarantee of land meant that there were no urban elites or large landowners supported by the agricultural production of others. The ancient Israelites saw this attempt to create an egalitarian society, both politically and economically, as embodying God's will for human social life.

Thus the event in which ancient Israel was born involved liberation from economic and political oppression and the creation of a nonhierarchical and nonexploitative social order under God. The exodus story is simultaneously religious and political, a tale of two lordships and two social visions: the lordship of Pharaoh and the lordship of God, the domination system of Egypt and the alternative social vision of Moses. As an epiphany of the dream of God, the story of the exodus has given an often ignored but ultimately indelible social and political dimension to the biblical, Jewish, and Christian traditions.

PEASANTS AND PROPHETS, KINGS AND ELITES

Israel's experiment with this social vision lasted a few hundred years. Then kingship arose within Israel itself around the year 1000 B.C.E. Within less than a hundred years the Israelite king and the emerging elites became the center of a new domination system. The king became in effect a new pharaoh, a development well under way in the reign of Solomon (965–922 B.C.E.). The social structures of preindustrial agrarian society were reestablished within Israel.

The conflict between the royal consciousness of Pharaoh and the alternative consciousness of Moses was now a conflict within ancient Israel itself. Two different theologies developed, both claiming to speak for the same God, both found in the Hebrew Bible. On one side were kings and elites; on the other, prophets and peasants.

Elite Theology

The theology of the elites was expressed in the royal theology of the Hebrew Bible. According to this theology, the king was a gift of God.[18] Anointed by God, he was "God's son," and to him and his descendants God had promised everlasting rule:

> I [God] will establish the throne of his kingdom forever. I will be a father to him, and he shall be a son to me. . . . Your dynasty, kingdom and throne shall be established forever.[19]

Royal theology was centered in the temple as well as in the king. God had promised to dwell in the temple forever, and the temple's presence in Jerusalem (the home of the king and the urban elites) divinely guaranteed the security of Jerusalem and the ruling order.

Prophetic Theology

In the name of the same God, the classical prophets of ancient Israel attacked the domination system and the theology of the elites legitimating it. Theirs were voices of religious social protest.[20] As God-intoxicated Spirit persons, they were impelled by their experience of the sacred to indict the elites for their exploitation of the poor. They also energized the imagination of their hearers with visions of a different social order. They were bearers and spokespersons of the dream of God.

Their social passion was unmistakable, their gifts of language extraordinary. Speaking in public places with powerful and memorable words, they radically criticized the ruling elites in the name of God's justice. In the eighth century B.C.E., Amos said to the elites:

> Woe to those who lie upon beds of ivory,
> and stretch themselves upon their couches,
> and eat lambs from the flock,
> and calves from the midst of the stall;
> who sing idle songs to the sound of the harp,
> and like David invent for themselves instruments of music;
> who drink wine in bowls,
> and anoint themselves with the finest oils,
> but they are not grieved over the ruin of Joseph [meaning the poor of
>   their peasant society].[21]

Amos's indictment continued:

You trample the head of the poor into the dust of the earth, and push the afflicted out of the way. . . .

You oppress the poor and crush the needy. . . .

You trample on the poor and take from them taxes of grain. . . .

You trample on the needy, and bring to ruin the poor of the land. . . .

You buy the poor for silver and the needy for a pair of sandals, and sell the sweepings of the wheat [as good grain].[22]

In the same century, Micah named the capital cities of the northern and southern kingdoms (Samaria and Jerusalem) as the "transgression" or "sin" of each kingdom:

What is the transgression of Jacob [the northern kingdom]?
Is it not Samaria?
And what is the sin of the house of Judah [the southern kingdom]?
Is it not Jerusalem?[23]

Why this naming of cities as the source of sin? Because they are the home of the urban elites; *that* is where the sin of the kingdoms resides.
About the elites Micah also said:

Listen, you heads of Jacob
and rulers of the house of Israel!
Should you not know justice—
you who hate the good and love the evil,
who tear the skin off *my people,* and the flesh off their bones;
who eat the flesh of *my people,*
flay their skin off them,
break their bones in pieces,
and chop them up like meat in a kettle,
like flesh in a caldron.[24]

"My people" (God's people) are the poor, the systemically oppressed and victimized.
About the elite's acquisition of land from peasants, Micah said:

They covet fields and seize them;
houses, and take them away;
they oppress householder and house,
people and their inheritance.[25]

Isaiah addressed Jerusalem and brilliantly used his song about the vineyard and all the owner (God) did to make it fruitful to lead his hearers to pass judgment on themselves. He concluded with four lines containing memorable wordplays in Hebrew:

> God looked for justice [mishpat],
> but behold, bloodshed [mishpa];
> for righteousness [sedaqah],
> but behold, a cry [se-aqah]![26]

Where God looked for justice and righteousness, there were instead (because of the elites) bloodshed and the cry of the afflicted.

Jeremiah found a similar absence of justice in the capital of the elites:

> Run to and fro through the streets of Jerusalem,
> Look and take note!
> Search her squares to see if you can find one man
> who does justice and seeks truth.[27]

He mocked the elites who appealed to the royal theology to legitimate their rule: "Do not trust in these deceptive words, 'This is the temple of the Lord, the temple of the Lord, the temple of the Lord.' "[28] Devotion and the recitation of pious theology will do no good.

What then did God want? In the name of God and speaking on God's behalf, Amos said:

> I hate, I despise your religious festivals;
> I take no delight in your solemn assemblies
> (or in your burnt offerings, or in the noise of your songs, or the melody of
>   your harps)
> *But let justice roll down like waters,*
> *and righteousness like an ever-flowing stream.*[29]

The prophet Micah imagined a person pondering what God wants:

> With what shall I come before the Lord,
> and bow myself before God on high?
> Shall I come before God with burnt offerings,
> with calves a year old?
> Will the Lord be pleased with thousands of rams,
> with ten thousands of rivers of oil?
> Shall I give my firstborn for my transgression,
> the fruit of my body for the sin of my soul?

Is that what God wants? Micah answered his own question:

> God has told you, O mortal, what is good,
> and what does the Lord require of you
> *but to do justice,*
> *and to love kindness,*
> *and to walk humbly with your God?*[30]

Do justice, love kindness, and walk humbly with God.[31]

The passion for social justice that we see in the prophets is a protest against systemic evil. Systemic evil is an important notion: it refers to the injustice built into the structures of the system itself. Embedded in oppressive and exploitative social structures, systemic evil is a major source (perhaps the single greatest cause) of human suffering.

Importantly, the issue is not the goodness or wickedness of elite individuals. Elites can be good people: devout, responsible, courageous; kind, gentle, charming, intelligent; committed to family, loyal to friends, and so forth. Moreover, systemic evil is not necessarily intended even by some who benefit from it. So the issue is not character flaws among the elites. The issue, rather, is a system in which some people sleep on beds made of ivory while others end up being sold for the price of a pair of sandals.

Thus the passion for social justice does not focus on individual change but on structural change. Of course, individual persons can be converted to a passion for justice (and such conversion is important), but when they are, their concern is not to maximize charitable giving within the existing structures but to change the structures themselves. The prophets were not simply saying to the elites, "Be good people, more charitable to the poor, and worship the right God." They said, in Amos's words, "Seek justice, and live." The problem was not individual sinfulness but a social system in which the poor of the land were brought to ruin.

JESUS AND THE DREAM OF GOD

The dream of God blazed forth again in Jesus. He lived in a peasant society under the kingship of Herod and the kingship of Caesar. The social world of the Jewish homeland in the first century was a two-tier domination system: a native domination system centered in the elites of Jerusalem and the temple, and the imperial domination system of Rome, to whom the native elites paid both allegiance and monetary tribute (extracted from peasant agricultural production).

In this setting, and in addition to being a Spirit person, healer, and wisdom teacher, Jesus was a social prophet. There was passion in his language. Many of his sayings (as well as actions) challenged the domination system of his day. They take on pointed meaning when we see them in the context of social criticism of a peasant society. His criticisms of the wealthy were an indictment of the social class at the top of the domination system. His prophetic threats against Jerusalem and the temple were not because they were the center of an "old religion" (Judaism) soon to be replaced by a new religion (Christianity) but because they were the center of the domination system. His criticism of lawyers, scribes, and Pharisees was not because they were unvirtuous individuals but because commitment to the elites led them to see the social order through elite lenses.

Jesus rejected the sharp social boundaries of the established social order and challenged the institutions that legitimated it. In his teaching, he subverted distinctions between righteous and sinner, rich and poor, men and women, Pharisee and outcasts. In his healings and behavior, he crossed social boundaries of purity, gender, and class. In his meal practice, central to what he was about, he embodied a boundary-subverting inclusiveness.

In his itinerancy he rejected the notion of a brokered kingdom of God and enacted the immediacy of access to God apart from institutional mediation. His prophetic act against the money changers in the temple at the center of the domination system was, in the judgment of most scholars, the trigger leading to his arrest and execution.

It is important not to domesticate Jesus' social passion. The point is not that Jesus was a good guy who accepted everybody, and thus we should do the same (though that *would* be good). Rather, his teachings and behavior reflect an alternative social vision. Jesus was not talking about how to be good and how to behave within the framework of a domination system. He was a critic of the domination system itself. Indeed, that's the best explanation for why he was killed. He wasn't simply a nice inclusive fellow but a religious social prophet whose teaching, behavior, and social vision radically challenged the elites and the domination system of his day.

The dream of God as we see it in Jesus—his alternative social vision—is usefully crystallized in three complementary ways. First, I call it a "politics of compassion."[32] For Jesus, compassion was more than a virtue for the individual. It was the basis of his criticism of the social order: for Jesus, the compassion of God stood against the domination system of his day. Compassion was also the paradigm or core value of his social vision: Jesus' understanding of God as compassionate led to a social vision grounded in compassion. It stood in sharp contrast to the core value of the social vision of elite theology, which was a politics of holiness and purity centered in the temple and legitimating the social order. Compassion as a core political paradigm suggests a political order that is life-giving, nourishing, and inclusive.

Second, the most effective shorthand nonbiblical language known to me for the dream of God and its opposition to elite theology and politics has been supplied by Walter Wink. Elite theology and politics lead to "domination systems." The opposite is "God's domination-free order."[33] This—God's "domination-free order"—is the dream of God. The exodus paradigm, which surfaced again in the prophets and Jesus, is meant for all of us. We are not meant to live under the domination of Pharaoh or Caesar, whatever form that takes.

Third, one may speak of Jesus' social vision with one of his most frequently used phrases: "the kingdom of God." Though the phrase had several nuances of meaning, one was theopolitical. His hearers knew about other kingdoms, especially Herod's and Caesar's. The kingdom of God is what the world would be like if God were king, rather than Herod or Caesar. In such a world, the poor would be fortunate, the mighty put down from their thrones, the rich sent away empty-handed. Domination systems would be replaced by God's domination-free order.[34]

Strikingly, we pray that this kingdom—God's kingdom—might come on earth every time we pray the Lord's Prayer: "Thy kingdom come, thy will be done *on earth* as it is in heaven." But we often miss the connection because of the cadence with which we most frequently pray this prayer: "Thy kingdom come, thy will be done" is separated by a single-beat pause from "on earth, as it is in heaven."[35] But the syntax is clear: we are praying for the coming of God's kingdom *on earth*. As Dominic Crossan comments: heaven is already in good shape; what we pray for is that the kingdom of God may also be on earth. [36] *That* is the dream of God.[37]

Thus, running throughout the biblical tradition is a conflict between two different social visions, two different understandings of God, two different theologies. Both claimed the same religious tradition, told the same stories, and used the same language. But each told the stories and used the tradition differently. The theology of the elites used the tradition to legitimate the existing order. The passionate champions of God's compassion challenged the present order and dreamed the dream of God.

Because I have emphasized the centrality of a just social order in the prophetic voices of the biblical tradition, I also want to underline the value of the individual in the same tradition. The Bible is not just about social justice and the shape of society. Individuals mattered to Jesus and to God. To use a phrase that sounds old-fashioned and that comes from an earlier generation of scholars, the Bible affirms the infinite value of the individual person.

But we should think of concern for the individual and concern for a just society not as an either-or choice but as a both-and. The prophetic voices of the tradition show a deep awareness of how individuals are victimized by society. Passion for the well-being of individuals and passion about the shape of the community go hand in hand. Because individuals matter to God, political structures matter to God, for political structures impact the lives of individuals to an exceptional degree. Thus the dream of God combines an emphasis on the value of the individual with a passionate concern for a just society.

THE DREAM OF GOD IN CHRISTIAN HISTORY

The dream of God has not fared well in Christian history. Beginning with the Roman emperor Constantine in the fourth century, the dream of God has most frequently been accommodated to the existing social order. Constantine not only legalized Christianity in the year 313 but to a considerable extent became its sponsor. Before the end of the same century, under one of his successors, Christianity had become the official religion of the empire.

Often this development is seen as the triumph of Christianity over the empire that had been its persecutor. But an equally good case can be made that the empire took over the church rather than the church taking over the empire. Indeed, Verna Dozier speaks of this development as the third major rejection of the dream of God.[38] Dominic Crossan makes a similar claim. He quotes the early church historian Eusebius's description of an imperial banquet hosted by Constantine in one of his palaces for the bishops of the church:

> Detachments of the bodyguard and troops surrounded the entrance of the palace with drawn swords, and through the midst of them the men of God [the bishops] proceeded without fear into the innermost of the Imperial apartments, in which some were the Emperor's companions at table, while others reclined on couches arranged on either side. One might have thought that a picture of Christ's kingdom was thus shadowed forth, and a dream rather than reality.[39]

Crossan comments: the inclusive meal practice of Jesus the social prophet has been replaced by an imperial banquet at which "the participants are the male bishops alone, and they recline, with the emperor himself, to be served by others. Dream or reality? Dream or nightmare?"[40]

For most of the centuries since, in lands where Christianity has been the primary religion, it has most often been allied with the established order. The dream of God has not been totally absent; it has surfaced occasionally in the lives of saints and reformers and movements. But God's dream has not been the dominant voice of the tradition.

THE DREAM OF GOD AND CONTEMPORARY AMERICAN SOCIETY

In the modern period, the alliance between Christianity and the political order continues to some extent. But even more so, the dream of God has been submerged by the individualism that characterizes much of modern Western culture. The dream of God is quite different from contemporary American dreams. The dream of God—a politics of compassion and justice, the kingdom of God, a domination-free order—is social, communal, and egalitarian. But our dreams—the dreams we get from our culture—are individualistic: living well, looking good, standing out.

The evidence for this claim is, in a sense, everywhere. We need only look around us to see the dreams that animate us. It is also the conclusion of a study of the central values of American society by Robert Bellah and his colleagues.[41] They argue that there are two major strands in the American cultural tradition. One strand emphasizes the importance of community, based on biblical and classical ideas of covenant and civic virtue. The other strand emphasizes the individual. Both strands are important and can be combined, as they sometimes have been in American history and as they are in the biblical tradition.

But according to Bellah and his colleagues, the individualistic strand has become dominant in our recent history, so that the core value or ethos of contemporary American society is individualism. Our quest—in our work, relationships, families, ambitions, organizations, often our religious practices—is the personal fulfillment of the individual, however we define that fulfillment.

In one of my classes, I engage my students in an exercise designed to put them in touch with "American conventional wisdom." I explain briefly what I mean by that phrase—namely, the central messages that we acquire simply from growing up in our culture. I then invite them to come up with short sayings that express messages they've gotten: contemporary American proverbs, slogans, advertising lines, visual images, or their own short crystallization of cultural messages.

Though not comprehensive, the following list is typical:

Be all that you can be.
Just do it.
Whoever dies with the most toys wins.
You only go around once.
Go for the gusto.
Look out for number one.
Work hard and you'll succeed.
Plan for retirement.
Life is about having and consuming.
Government is bad.
Be slender (fit, strong, sensitive).
Enjoy yourself.
Nice guys finish last.
Seek fame and fortune.

None of these is a community value. Once in a while, my students will suggest the Golden Rule, or love your neighbor as yourself, but that's about it. They report no messages about working for a just society, or having an obligation to future generations, or building the kingdom of God on earth.[42] Their responses confirm Bellah and his colleagues' analysis of our individualistic ethos.

The individualism of contemporary American culture affects us in many ways. It affects the way Christianity is understood. For many Christians, the significant religious issues concern the individual, whether those issues are salvation in an afterlife, or individual righteousness, or peace of mind, or personal spiritual development in the present. Individualism leads to an individualistic interpretation of the Bible. Passages such as "the poor you will always have with you" or "whoever does not work shall not eat" are much better known than prophetic passages about justice.[43] Jesus' saying, "Render to Caesar that which is Caesar's, and to God that which is God's" is frequently understood as establishing two separate realms—a public one of politics and economics and a private one of religion and God.[44]

A Politics of Individualism

When contemporary American Christians do become political, they tend to remain individualistic in their thinking. Among the "religious right," the most visible form of Christian politics today, the central political issues concern individual behavior. Many involve sexuality: abortion, pornography, homosexuality. The issue of "welfare mothers" often becomes an issue of sexual morality, and the welfare debate becomes a debate about family values. The political vision of the religious right is for the most part an individualistic politics of righteousness, not a communal politics of compassion.[45]

Beyond Christian circles, our ethos of individualism pervasively affects our political life. When we think about politics, we think individualistically. The reason the poor are poor is because of individual failings, not because of social and economic policy. The solution is individualistic as well: the poor need to develop a work ethic and embrace family values. Antigovernment sentiment and the tax revolt also reflect the triumph of individual values over community values: we think we shouldn't have to pay taxes for the well-being of the community as a whole.

Our individualism affects the way we think about justice. As Bellah and his colleagues point out, we emphasize procedural justice much more than substantive or distributive justice. Indeed, our emphasis on the former has almost eclipsed the latter. The former is concerned with the rights of individuals and the fair enforcement of rules (and the protection of individual rights is one of the glories of the American political tradition), the latter with the question of what a just society is. The former is concerned with maximizing opportunities for individuals, the latter with a social vision centered in community and not just in the rights of competing individuals.[46]

Our ethos and politics of individualism affect our economic life, generating a society with increasingly sharp social boundaries based on wealth. There are other important social boundaries as well, including race, gender, sexual orientation, age, and physical ability. But we have made progress in all of these areas in the second half of this century. Though all require continued attention and vigilance, I do not know anybody who would say we are worse off now in these areas than we were at midcentury.

But social boundaries based on wealth have become sharper. The United States over the last thirty years has seen a growing gap—indeed, a deepening gulf—between rich and poor.[47] The gap is significantly greater than in any other developed nation.[48] Moreover, the growing gulf between rich and poor is the result of social and economic policy, not because some classes of people worked harder and others slacked off over the last thirty years (all of us, according to most studies, are working harder). The differences among countries generate the same conclusion: social policy, not simply individual effort, is responsible for the distribution of wealth. Our recent social policy may not have been intended to produce this result, but it has. The consequence is increased suffering and desperation among the poor and potentially grave consequences for the society as a whole.[49]

Moreover, many people in the middle, who are most often struggling financially, support the individualistic ideology underlying our social policy—namely, the notions that we each have worked hard for what we have and ought to be able to keep all of it, that government is bad (or at least inefficient and wasteful—and hungry for our tax dollars), and that things will be better for all of us if we let the wealthiest people in our country make and keep as much money as possible. Many of us seem not to realize that the people who benefit the most from our politics and economics of individualism are the wealthiest 10 percent, especially the top 1 percent. People will support a tax cut that saves them $300 a year, without considering that the same tax cut will save the very wealthy tens of thousands or even hundreds of thousands a year, with significant damage to the social fabric, including not only decreased help for the poor and disadvantaged but also cuts in services such as public schools, road repairs, parks, libraries, and so forth.

Thus our culture's ethos of individualism generates a political ideology benefiting elites in particular. It legitimates their place in society: if you have prospered, it's because you have worked hard and made good use of your opportunities; you deserve what you've got. It legitimates social and economic policies that increase private wealth and generate public poverty. It legitimates blaming the poor. The conclusion strikes me as compelling: we have an elite-driven social and economic policy.[50]

This indictment of an elite-driven social policy is not an indictment of the American middle class.[51] I am not suggesting that there is something morally culpable about having a comfortable home, or two cars, or an annual vacation, or a CD collection, or a pension. One would wish that level of comfort and security for everybody (with, of course, appropriate environmental thoughtfulness). The point is not that there is something morally wrong with a middle-class standard of living. Rather, the issue is the political values and attitudes that are widespread in our culture (including among the middle class) and the need to change our politics of individualism to a politics that recognizes the indispensability of community. The appropriate response is not "feeling guilty about what I have" but a different political vision.

Christians, the Church, and the Dream of God

What is the relevance of the dream of God—the kingdom of God on earth—in our situation? What would it mean to take seriously the cumulative witness of Moses, Jesus, and the prophets? What might a politics of compassion and justice have to say to us?

Taking seriously the dream of God would mean seeing a political dimension to the Christian life. Grounded in God's compassion for suffering people, including those pressed down and marginalized by the structures of society, a politics of compassion leads to a very different way of seeing human life in community.

A POLITICS OF COMPASSION

I begin with a clarifying remark about compassion. It strikes some people as a "weak" value, particularly in the context of politics.[52] Thus it is important to underline that compassion does not mean simply being "nice." Nor does it mean "letting people off the hook," as if one would say in every situation, "I understand," and never hold anybody accountable. The strength of compassion as a value can be seen by looking at its opposites: hatred, abuse, brutality, injustice; indifference, selfishness, self-righteousness (in religious or secular form), hardness of heart; racism, sexism, classism, militant nationalism, and so forth. To advocate compassion is to stand against these. Thus it is not a "weak" value that tolerates everything.

What difference might it make to adopt a politics of compassion, grounded in the compassion of God? Enacting the kingdom of God on earth is a utopian vision, an ideal. Yet it seems to me that it has what the American theologian and social ethicist Reinhold Niebuhr in the first half of this century called "the relevance of an impossible ideal."[53] The goal is to approximate the egalitarian and inclusive social vision of the kingdom of God in history; the fact that we cannot perfectly embody it does not mean that it should cease to be an ideal.

It is important to realize that compassion as a political value is a paradigm. Paradigms are not policies; instead, paradigms affect the way we see and provide a framework for our thinking. Compassion as a political paradigm is both a "lens" for seeing and the "core value" of an alternative way of thinking about society. Thus a politics of compassion is not a particular set of specific economic and social policies but a social vision that is to affect all of our political thinking. How best to implement and incarnate that vision is to a large extent a pragmatic question of what works best to reach that goal.[54]

As a political paradigm, what might compassion lead us to see? As the biblical vision of a domination-free order, the dream of God, the kingdom of God on earth, what does a politics of compassion imply for Christian perception of and relationship to the social order?

It leads to seeing the impact of social structures on people's lives. It leads to seeing that the economic suffering of the poor is not primarily due to individual failure. It leads to seeing that the categories of "marginal," "inferior," and "outcast" are human impositions. It leads to anger toward the sources of human suffering, whether individual or systemic.

It leads to advocacy of a different social vision. As the word *compassion* itself suggests, a politics of compassion seeks a life-giving, inclusive social order. The focus of a politics of compassion is the alleviation of suffering caused by social structures. It leads to minimizing social boundaries, whatever the basis for drawing them (status, wealth, gender, race, sexual orientation, and so forth). Positively, it seeks to create social structures that are stewards of nourishment for the society as a whole, rather than channels funneling benefits to a relatively few.

As an ideal tempered by realism about the human condition, a politics of compassion does not mean the complete absence of hierarchies and authority structures. We could not live together in groups without them. Nor, under the conditions of history, does it mean an absence of income differentials.

But a politics of compassion would affect how we think about such matters. Two sets of questions illustrate the difference that a shift in paradigms from a politics of individualism to a politics of compassion would make.

First, how does one care for the victims of the system? Advocates of a politics of individualism commonly answer, "Through private charity"—what a former president called "a thousand points of light." Of course, private charity is important, but this response ignores the fact that in modern American society, with the disappearance of traditional communities, government social policy is the primary way of caring for people we do not know. Advocates of a politics of compassion thus would ask, "How can we change the structures so that there aren't as many victims?"

Second, how does one balance rewards for individual initiative with a compassionate social order? Advocates of a politics of individualism would think about it this way: How, within a politics of incentives and rewards, does one find a place for compassion? Advocates of a politics of compassion would start at the other end and ask, instead: How, within a politics of compassion, does one recognize the importance of incentives and rewards for individual initiative?

The church as the community of Jesus is called to incarnate the inclusive and egalitarian social vision of Jesus in its internal life. In its own polity, it is to be a community of compassion. It is to embody the inclusive social vision of which Paul spoke, which negated the sharpest social boundaries of his time: "In Christ, there is neither Jew nor Gentile, slave nor free, male nor female."[55] Paul's list should not be seen as exhaustive or comprehensive but as examples of the boundaries overcome "in Christ."

Moreover, the church as the community of Jesus is called not only to a polity of compassion but to a politics of compassion. The church is to be the leaven of compassion in the world. In our time, becoming the leaven of compassion means consciousness-raising in local congregations about the social vision of the great voices of the biblical tradition, about the way social structures impact people's lives, and about the contrast between compassion as a social vision and today's dominant political ethos.

What does a community committed to a different paradigm (compassion) and living by a different imperative (the dream of God) do in a cultural situation such as our own? Do we dare, in our time and in the church, to talk about elite-driven politics? Are we persuaded that's the case? Do we dare to say that social policies are central to becoming a more compassionate society? Are we willing to consider that economic policy is the central political question of our time? How large do we think the gap between the richest 10 percent of our population and the poorest 10 percent should be? And is that a decision for the community, the body politic, to make, rather than a decision to leave to the elites? Just as we as Christians need to learn how to pray, so also we need to learn how to see and think and live compassionately.

The Christian life involves a journey inward (the hatching of the heart) and a journey outward. Our journey outward as followers of Jesus, as advocates of the dream of God, as the church, calls us to be a community of compassion and the leaven of compassion in the world. We are called to compassion not just as an individual virtue but to compassion in our political thinking.

Such is the dream of God: a politics of compassion, the kingdom of God on earth. I am enough of a realist to think that we will never achieve the kingdom of God on earth—but there are approximations. It is that dream that so many voices in the biblical tradition speak of: justice rolling down like waters; the lamb lying down with the lion; the earth as the pasture of God; a time when we will beat our swords into plowshares, when the hills will drip with honey, and the mountains run with wine, when the covenant with God will be written on our hearts, and when every tear will be wiped away, and there will be no grief or sorrow anymore.

Ultimately, as the last line in the preceding paragraph from the great concluding vision of the book of Revelation suggests, the dream of God takes us beyond history. But I am convinced that the dream of God is for history as well. It is a dream for this earth.

Notes

1. Amos, eighth century B.C.E.

2. The last half of the sentence is from Paul in Rom. 13.7. It is highly unlikely that Paul intended this as a "blank-check" endorsement of political authority.

3. Christian spirituality is neither intrinsically nor properly individualistic, yet it is easily co-opted by individualism, especially in a culture such as our own. See Leech, *The Eye of the Storm*.

4. See Stephen Carter's use of the phrase "God as a hobby" in *The Culture of Disbelief* (New York: Basic Books, 1993), pp. 23–43.

5. Verna Dozier, *The Dream of God: A Call to Return* (Boston: Cowley, 1991).

6. Micah 4.4. For people to sit under their own fig tree and vine is a symbol of everybody being secure and having his or her own parcel of land, with ample food; see also Isa. 36.16 and Zech. 3.10.

7. Isa. 2.4b. Also found in Micah 4.3b, suggesting that it was a saying widely known in prophetic circles.

8. Amos 9.13. This is a vision of prosperity for everybody.

9. Gerhard Lenski, *Power and Privilege: A Theory of Social Stratification* (New York: McGraw-Hill, 1966).

10. Though most peasants were agricultural producers, the peasant class also included fishers, artisans, herders, miners, beggars, and so forth.

11. These figures are averages, based on Lenski's study of several societies *(Power and Privilege)*. Even if the percentages were quite different in some peasant societies, the basic picture would remain: a small elite living in considerable luxury, while the mass of people were rural producers. This was the pattern in any premodern society that had an aristocracy.

12. The biblical "three score and ten" as a common span for a good life reflects the vantage point of elites. Life spans for elites have not changed that much over time. Peasant life expectancy was more like twenty-five.

13. For the phrase "domination system" (and its opposite, "domination-free order"), I am indebted to Walter Wink's important and illuminating book, *Engaging the Powers*.

14. This is a close paraphrase of Walter Brueggemann's language in *The Prophetic Imagination* (Philadelphia: Fortress, 1978), pp. 32–43.

15. Exod. 2.23–24.

16. Exod. 3.7.

17. This is the picture generated by the books of Joshua and Judges. We do not know whether the picture of equal land distribution is idealized to some degree.

18. 1 Sam. 9.16, 10.1. Interestingly, 1 Sam. 8 paints a very different picture: the Israelites' request for a king displeases God and is the source of their future problems. The pro-king and anti-king attitudes of these two chapters of 1 Samuel reflect the conflict between the two theologies.

19. 2 Sam. 7.13–14, 16. See also Ps. 89, esp. verses 3–4, 27–37; and in Ps. 2.7, the king is God's "son."

20. They were *social prophets* rather than *predictors* of a distant future, a point I emphasize because of the widespread Christian misunderstanding of the classical prophets of the Hebrew Bible that sees them primarily as foretellers (predictors) of the Messiah (namely, Jesus). This misunderstanding is rooted in the way prophetic passages are often used in the New Testament (especially Matthew). But in their original historical setting, the prophets were not foreseers of events in the distant future or predictors of the Messiah. Rather, in the name of God, they indicted the injustices of the present, threatened the elites with destruction, and urged an alternative future.

21. Amos 6.4–6.

22. In sequence: Amos 2.7, 4.1, 5.11, 8.4, 8.6.

23. Micah 1.5b.

24. Micah 3.1–3.

25. Micah 2.2.

26. Isa. 5.1–7, with climax in 7b.

27. Jer. 5.1.

28. Jer. 7.4.

29. Amos 5:21 (22–23), 24. These were not pagan religious festivals; they honored the God of Israel. The point seems to be that religious observance without social justice is meaningless (indeed, hateful) to God.

30. Micah 6.6–8.

31. Walking *humbly* with God is the opposite of having a hard or arrogant heart. See Chapter Five in this book.

32. See especially *Meeting Jesus Again,* Chapter Three, and *Jesus in Contemporary Scholarship,* Chapter Five.

33. Wink, *Engaging the Powers.*

34. For this understanding of kingdom, see especially Crossan, *Jesus: A Revolutionary Biography,* pp. 54–122; *The Historical Jesus,* pp. 225–53; and Wink, *Engaging the Powers,* pp. 109–37.

35. Verna Dozier pointed this out to me in conversation. I do not believe she makes this comment in her book.

36. Crossan makes this point in several of his books and most recently in his essay in *Jesus at 2000,* "Jesus and the Kingdom," pp. 52–53.

37. As I write about the kingdom of God *on earth,* I am aware of how utopian it sounds (perhaps accentuated by my Lutheran and Republican childhood). My practical side comes out later in the chapter.

38. Dozier, *The Dream of God.* The first rejection of the dream was the primal existential turning away from God in the Garden of Eden story; the second rejection was the rise of the monarchy in Israel.

39. Eusebius, *Life of Constantine* 3.15, cited by Crossan, *Jesus: A Revolutionary Biography,* p. 201.

40. Crossan, *Jesus,* p. 201.

41. Robert Bellah, Richard Madsen, William Sullivan, Ann Swidler, and Steven Tipton, *Habits of the Heart: Individualism and Commitment in American Life* (Berkeley: University of California Press, rev. ed. 1996; originally published in 1985) and *The Good Society* (New York: Knopf, 1991).

42. My point is not that none of my students might think these are important but that they do not report them as messages they've gotten.

43. Mark 14.7 and 2 Thess. 3.10.

44. Mark 12.13. As words of Jesus, the saying did not mean this. It functioned in part to discredit his opponents and in part as a way of evading a "trap" question. Whether it had a positive meaning as well—and if so, what that might be—are probably impossible to know. The crucial factor is *what* belongs to Caesar and *what* belongs to God. One could read it as implying the question, "Does *any-thing* rightfully belong to Caesar?" I am not arguing that this was its original meaning; rather, I am pointing out that the positive meaning of the saying is enigmatic at best.

45. My impressions of the Christian right are those of an outsider, formed from reading and from Christian radio and television. Though conservative theology and conservative politics often go together, they do not always. A striking example is the evangelist Tony Campolo; though his theology is conservative-evangelical, he has a passionate commitment to a politics of compassion. In a fea-

ture on National Public Radio's *All Things Considered* in October 1996, he echoed the words of Jesus in Matthew 25 as he imagined our generation being interrogated at the last judgment: "Did you feed the hungry?" "No, but we balanced the budget." "Did you clothe the naked?" "No, but we cut taxes."

46. Bellah and others, *Habits of the Heart*, pp. 25–26, 29, 31, 334 (page numbers refer to 1985 edition).

47. Three sets of statistics illustrate the point and disclose a striking direction in our national life. Being thoughtful about any one of them suggests that our social policies are driven by elite interests and serve elite ends. (1) During the 1980s, 90 percent of the total increase in income went to the wealthiest 20 percent of the population. The bottom 80 percent made do with the remaining 10 percent increase. (2) In 1963, the ratio of CEO salaries to average worker salaries in the same company was 41:1. Now, the ratio is 225:1. (In Germany, to provide a comparison, the ratio is 20:1). (3) In 1963, the wealthiest 1 percent of families owned 23 percent of all family assets (houses, cars, furniture, stocks and bonds, savings, and so on). In 1994, the wealthiest 1 percent of families owned 44 percent.

48. In the United States, the ratio of annual income received by the top 10 percent of the population compared to the bottom 10 percent is six to one. In Finland, it is just over two to one; in France, two-and-one-half to one; in Germany and the United Kingdom, three to one.

49. The separation between rich and poor is becoming more visible and more built in to the structures of society. Schools in urban areas reflect it, both because schools are neighborhood-based, as are poverty and wealth, and because of the growth of private schools. The separation is also seen in the growth of gated communities in many urban areas, usually with their own private security forces. Our gated communities recall the way elites lived in preindustrial societies: in walled cities, closed off from the masses of people. Of course, gated communities reflect fear about crime and violence in our society. Our crime rate and percentage of population in prison are higher than those of any other developed country. Why is that? Are individuals simply more criminally minded here? Or is it (as seems far more likely to me) a consequence of social structure?

50. This should not surprise us. In every society (at least since the development of agriculture and cities), elites have sought to use social policy to serve their own interests. If there are exceptions, praise the Lord, and let us learn from them.

51. It is hard to know how to define the American middle class in financial terms, especially if one adds in lower middle class and upper middle class. About two years ago, a member of Congress from Texas, while denying that a proposed tax cut would benefit primarily the wealthy and not the middle class, defined the middle class as people making between $300,000 to $700,000 a year (I do not know if he has been reelected). Needless to say, this is ridiculous. But incomes that a few decades ago would have made one rich are now middle class. It is not unusual for a working couple, both of whom are middle-income professionals, to have a combined income of $100,000 a year. I think of the middle class roughly as people whose income puts them somewhere between the fortieth and ninetieth income percentiles of our population (about $40,000 to $100,000 a year).

52. For example, I have been asked several times whether compassion in the political arena would mean that nobody should ever be imprisoned. The questioners were not advocating this but were either confusing compassion with mercy or seeking to show that compassion cannot be a political value.

53. A major theme in Niebuhr's writing, it is developed especially in his *An Interpretation of Christian Ethics* (New York: Harper and Brothers, 1935).

54. I am not a political theorist or economist, so I have no expertise in the area of specific social and economic policies. My impression, however, is that in our time a "mixed economy" incorporating elements of free enterprise can best serve the ends of a politics of compassion.

55. Gal. 3.28.

CHAPTER 7

SALVATION:

WHAT ON EARTH DO WE MEAN?[1]

My understanding of the meaning of salvation has changed radically over the course of my life. The revisioning of Christianity described throughout this book has also included a new understanding—which is also ancient—of this central Christian word.

Salvation and the afterlife have been closely linked in popular Christianity throughout the centuries. The first meaning listed under "salvation" in *The Oxford English Dictionary* is "the saving of the soul; the deliverance from sin and its consequences, and admission to eternal bliss."[2] So I thought when I was young, as mentioned earlier. Salvation concerned "Where will you spend eternity?" The question "Are you saved?" meant "Do you believe you will go to heaven when you die?"

Two closely related ideas were associated with this postdeath understanding of salvation. One was the notion of requirements. There was something we needed to do or believe in order to go to heaven. For me in my branch of the Christian tradition, the emphasis was on "faith" as the central requirement. For others, the emphasis may have been on good deeds or on some combination of faith and good deeds. But something was required; there had to be some basis for the eternal separation of sheep from goats at the last judgment. Second, salvation as afterlife was the primary reason for being a Christian. Otherwise, why bother? Words I recently saw on a T-shirt put it well: "Jesus is the only fire escape."

As the title of this chapter suggests, I now see matters differently. I am convinced that salvation in the biblical tradition has to do primarily with this life. This statement does not imply a denial of an afterlife, a topic to which I will return near the end of this chapter. But it now seems clear to me that salvation centrally concerns our life in this world.

SALVATION ON EARTH

I begin with an important historical observation about the meaning of salvation in the Bible. Namely, the notion of an afterlife appears only late in ancient Israel's history. The first explicit unambiguous reference to life after death is in the last chapter of the book of Daniel, written around the year 165 B.C.E.[3] Earlier books of the Bible either do not mention it or do so only ambiguously.[4] Clearly, it was not central. To provide some reference points: the stories of Abraham and Sarah, the father and mother of Israel, are set around the year 1700 B.C.E.; the exodus from Egypt occurred around 1300 B.C.E.; and the classical prophets spoke from about 750 to 400 B.C.E.

Through all of these centuries, the people of ancient Israel seem not to have believed in life after death. This means that for most of the biblical period, ancient Israel's life with God was not motivated by hope of an afterlife. Yet they spoke and wrote about salvation and the importance of taking God seriously.

Thus the primary biblical understanding of salvation is this-worldly, not otherworldly. This emphasis continues in the New Testament, even though the New Testament also affirms an afterlife. Salvation has to do with something that happens in this life. And so we ask: What on earth does salvation mean?

SALVATION AND THE WOUNDS OF EXISTENCE

An initial clue is provided by the linguistic root of the English word. *Salvation* comes from the same root as "salve," a healing ointment. Salvation thus has to do with healing the wounds of existence. This is no small matter, for the wounds of existence are many and deep. Some of these wounds are inflicted on us, some are the result of our own doing, and some we inflict on others.

The Bible uses a large number of images to suggest the meanings of salvation. Salvation in the Bible has both a divine and a human aspect: salvation comes from God, and salvation is something that we experience. The biblical images of salvation thus say something about God as well as about us. In the evocative language of metaphor, these images speak of God's involvement with us, as well as about what the experience of salvation is like.

BIBLICAL IMAGES OF SALVATION

Biblical images of salvation are correlated with images of the woundedness or predicament from which we need healing or deliverance. Metaphors are like families: they have relationships. We shall now consider a number of biblical images of salvation and the image of the human condition that goes with each. Cumulatively, they speak powerfully of our predicament—our woundedness—and of the salvation brought about through life with God.

Bondage and Liberation

Salvation as liberation goes back to the foundational narrative of the Bible, the exodus story of Israel's liberation from bondage in Egypt. Bondage as an image of the human predicament in this story includes economic and political oppression: the Hebrews were literally slaves under the lordship of Pharaoh. The image of our condition as bondage also has psychological and spiritual meanings in the Bible. For Paul, our bondage includes bondage to "the law," not as a nuisance or inconvenience and not to Jewish laws in particular but to "the law" as a way of defining our relationship to God. More comprehensively in Paul and the New Testament, we are in bondage to "the powers." "The powers" are cultural, spiritual, and psychological powers operating both within us and outside us. The powers include the domination system and the spirit of the age, and they produce in us not only bondage but a sense of powerlessness. Life under the powers is dominated existence.[5]

What does bondage suggest as an image of the human condition? We are in bondage to many things. Our bondage can be the result of things that happen to us, or we can fall into it through our own acts. Cultural messages are deeply ingrained within us, as are belief systems that radically shape the way we see and live. People continue to be in bondage to economic and political systems—both the victims of such systems as well as those who benefit from them (though in quite different ways). We can be in bondage to wounds stemming from childhood. We are addicted to many things. We typically are in bondage to preoccupation with ourselves and our well-being. The list can grow very long.

Liberation from bondage is thus one of the central meanings of salvation. The story of the exodus is a story about all of us and our need to be liberated from what holds us in bondage. Liberation is a central theme in the story of Jesus. According to Luke, Jesus' mission (then and now) is "to proclaim release to the captives, and to let the oppressed go free."[6] The language of liberation also resounds in the writings of Paul: "For freedom Christ has set us free . . . therefore, do not submit again to a yoke of slavery."[7] For Paul, God in Christ has defeated the powers, exposing and dethroning the other lords of our lives.

Estrangement and Reconciliation

A second biblical image of salvation is reconciliation: to be brought back into good relations after an estrangement. Estrangement is thus the corresponding image of the human condition, and it points to both relationship and separation: to be estranged is to be separated from that to which we belong.[8]

The central biblical image for the condition of estrangement is "exile." It is associated especially with the exile experience of the ancient Hebrews in Babylon in the sixth century B.C.E. There they sat down and wept when they remembered Jerusalem; there they felt abandoned by God; there they mourned and grieved. Exile is also the image of human existence in the story of the primal man and primal woman expelled from the Garden of Eden in the opening chapters of Genesis: we live our lives east of Eden, outside the manifest presence of God.

The image provocatively suggests that our lives are exilic. To be in exile is to be separated from that which one once knew, which feels like home, and for which one yearns. To be in exile involves living in an alien land under an alien lord. Like the exodus metaphor of bondage in Egypt, life in exile can have political and cultural meanings as well as psychological and spiritual ones. People in exile often experience oppression and powerlessness (though not always: one can become rich and powerful in exile if one lives there long enough). Life in exile commonly involves grief and sadness and sometimes anger and hostility. A virtual psychological synonym is alienation, which means to feel foreign. To be alienated is to feel oneself a stranger to oneself, to others, to life itself. Alienation involves feeling cut off from a center of meaning; it is the psychological effect of estrangement from God. Like bondage, exile is something that happens to us as well as something that we fall into or deepen by our own actions.

Salvation as reconciliation is the experience of being reconnected to God. It involves the overcoming of our sense of separation from the one to whom we belong. It is to return to Eden, symbolically the place of God's presence, to "paradise restored." It is homecoming. In the exile story, the process involves a journey of return to "the holy land," which (like Eden) is the place of God's presence. Indeed, this is one of the central meanings of "repentance" in the Bible: to repent means to return from exile to God. But this journey is not simply something that we do or accomplish, for God invites, encourages, and empowers the return.[9] So also in the New Testament: reconciliation is the work of God, as well as something we experience. According to Paul, God in Christ was reconciling the world to God, thereby making our own reconciliation to God possible.[10] The reconciling work of God also brings about reconciliation with one another, breaking down the walls of separation and hostility.[11]

Salvation as Enlightenment

Enlightenment is another image for salvation. We commonly associate "enlightenment" with Asian religions, but images of blindness and seeing, darkness and light, abound in the biblical and Christian tradition. Though we have eyes, we often do not see. We typically are blind to the glory of God all around us; we do not see each other as God sees us, and we do not see ourselves as God sees us. We are "in the dark," living in the night even when it is daytime. In the night, we cannot easily see, and we stumble or get lost. Night and darkness connect to fear and loneliness: we are often afraid in the dark and feel alone in the night. The night can be cold. It is also associated with death: things die without light. And it is a place of yearning: we yearn for the coming of the light like those watching for the morning.[12]

It is no wonder that the biblical tradition speaks so often of seeing and of the coming of the light:

> Arise, shine, for your light has come. . . . Darkness covers the earth, and thick darkness the peoples; but God will arise upon you . . . and nations shall come to the light.[13]

> The people who walked in darkness have seen a great light; those who dwell in a land of deep darkness, on them has light shined.[14]

> The day shall dawn from on high to give light to those who sit in darkness and in the shadow of death.[15]

> Thy word is a lamp unto my feet and a light to my path.[16]

> I [Jesus] am the light of the world; whoever follows me will not walk in darkness, but will have the light of life.[17]

> And the city [the new Jerusalem] has no need of sun or moon to shine upon it. . . . For night shall be no more; they need no light of lamp or sun, for the Lord God will be their light.[18]

> Once I was blind, but now I see.[19]

In the climactic dialogue of the book of Job, Job exclaims to God, "I had heard of you with the hearing of the ear, *but now my eye sees you.*"[20] The urgent request of the blind beggar Bartimaeus is the petition of all of us: "I want to see again."[21] According to the gospels, Jesus is the source of light and sight. In John's gospel, Jesus is "the light of the world" that "shines in the darkness, and the darkness has not overcome it."[22] Indeed, John speaks of Jesus as the true light that brings enlightenment: "The true light that enlightens everyone was coming into the world."[23] Salvation is enlightenment: the opening of our eyes to the presence and glory of God in the world, in each other, and in ourselves.

Salvation as Forgiveness

Salvation as the overcoming of our sin and guilt is another central image in the Christian tradition. Indeed, in popular-level Christianity over the centuries, the dynamic of sin and forgiveness has been the central issue of the Christian life: we have sinned against God, deserve judgment, and need forgiveness. But it seems to me that the importance of sin has often been overrated. Moreover, an emphasis on sin and guilt leads to a distorted and increasingly unpersuasive understanding of what being a Christian is about.

To be colloquial: this is a tricky one—primarily because there are two kinds of sin and guilt. There is an enculturated sense of sin and guilt that has little or nothing to do with God. The messages of our socialization (religious and secular) get internalized within our psyches as the critical voice of the superego, the police officer and judge in our head. Life under the superego is intrinsically a life of sin and guilt: we frequently fail to measure up to what our critical voice requires. There is thus what might be called false guilt or inauthentic guilt, imposed on us by socialization and reinforced by the monarchical model of God.[24] When this is the cause of feelings of sin and guilt, what is needed is not forgiveness but the replacement of a misleading image of God (the monarchical model) by a more truthful image of God. Our genuine need is not to hear that God the police officer and judge will let us off if we say we're really sorry but to hear that God is not primarily a police officer and judge.

But there is also real or authentic sin and guilt. We wound each other and ourselves through both deeds of commission and omission. We often do terrible things to each other. Some of these are willful acts: we could have done otherwise, but we chose not to. Some are the result of our blindness, bondage, and alienation. But whatever the mixture of causes, the result is that we often injure and even destroy each other.

For both our enculturated sense of sin and guilt and our authentic sin and guilt, the meaning of salvation as forgiveness is "You are accepted." This is one of the central meanings of grace in the Christian tradition: God accepts us just as we are. No "if" statement follows, despite our tendency to add one or more: we are accepted *if* we truly repent, *if* we truly believe, and so on. But adding an "if" statement makes our acceptance conditional and turns forgiveness into a reward for meeting a requirement. Rather, the message of forgiveness is unconditional grace: "You are accepted," period, full stop.[25]

Unconditional grace is a difficult notion for many people, including many Christians, for at least two reasons. First, it violates both religious and secular conventional wisdom, according to which there has to be a requirement: "You don't get something for nothing." Second, our difficulty also flows from commonly thinking of sin, forgiveness, and salvation within an afterlife framework. If God accepts everybody, does that not mean that everybody goes to heaven, regardless of how good or bad, repentant or unrepentant, faithful or unfaithful they are? And if so, why care about any of this?

But the mistake lies in thinking of sin and forgiveness within the framework of an afterlife. The issue is not making sure that one has adequately repented before one dies so that one's entry into heaven is not obstructed by unforgiven sins. Rather, salvation as forgiveness has powerful meaning for our life on earth: to know God's unconditional acceptance profoundly changes our sense of ourselves and our sense of what our lives are about. God loves me, in spite of what the critical voice within me says. God loves me in spite of my sense of sin and guilt.

To know this means that the Christian life is not about meeting God's requirements; that has been taken care of.[26] Rather, the Christian life is about living our lives in a relationship with the God who already accepts us and about letting the transforming power of the relationship with God work in our lives.

Of course, if one does not see this—namely, that one is already forgiven and accepted—then nothing changes: we remain burdened by sin and guilt and the life of measuring up. But to know God's unconditional acceptance is one of the most liberating experiences there is. No wonder one of the most moving hymns in the Christian tradition speaks of "amazing grace" that "saved a wretch like me; I once was lost, but now am found, was blind but now I see."

Salvation as Experiencing the Love of God

This understanding of salvation is closely related, though not identical, to that of salvation as forgiveness. It is similar in that it involves a transformation in self-understanding from "condemned" or "rejected" to "beloved of God." But knowing the love of God can also heal other wounds. Some people have a sense of being worthless, of little account, unlovely and loveless. For such people, salvation means being able to hear and internalize Isaiah's words about how God regards us: "You are precious in my eyes, and honored, and I love you."[27] To know that one is not worthless but precious, not unlovely and loveless but beloved by God, is a salvific experience. To know, as Roberta Bondi puts it, that God is besotted with us changes everything.[28]

Salvation as Resurrection

Resurrection in the New Testament sometimes refers to a future state beyond physical death. But it is also a metaphor for salvation in the midst of this life. It is closely related to the images of new birth or being born again, both of which belong to the same metaphorical family.

For this image of salvation, death has a twofold meaning. On the one hand, death is the corresponding image of the human condition: we can be "dead" in the midst of life. Jesus spoke of people who live in the land of the dead when he said, "Leave the dead to bury the dead."[29] The letters to the Ephesians and Colossians speak of people being "dead in their trespasses and sins."[30] Just as there are people who do not see even though they have eyes, who are asleep even though awake, so there are also people who are dead even though alive.

On the other hand, death is also a metaphor for the means of entry into resurrection life. One must die to an old way of being in order to enter a new way of being. Indeed, a widespread early Christian interpretation of the death and resurrection of Jesus saw it as the embodiment of this internal psychological and spiritual process. Paul spoke of himself as one who had experienced it: "I have been crucified with Christ; it is no longer I who live, but Christ who lives in me."[31] Paul also spoke of this as a process for all Christians: our old selves are to be crucified so that we might be raised with Christ and walk in newness of life. In John's gospel, Jesus is "the resurrection and the life," as well as "the way" that leads to new life in the present.[32] Salvation is resurrection to a new way of being here and now.

Salvation as Food and Drink

Images of food and drink are common in the biblical tradition. In the story of the exodus, God fed the Israelites in the wilderness with manna from the sky and satisfied their thirst with water from the rock. Using the language of thirst and hunger, the anonymous prophet of the exile said to his hearers, "Ho, everyone who thirsts, come to the waters; and you that have no money, come, buy and eat!" In Proverbs, Sophia the wisdom woman hosts a banquet of bread and wine: "Come, eat of my bread and drink of the wine I have mixed."[33]

The metaphorical use of hunger and thirst can be very powerful. We hunger, often even when we are satiated; we feel empty and long for something more, even though our stomachs may be full. We thirst as if we live in an arid and desert wasteland, our throats dry like parchment.

The metaphorical use of food and drink, hunger and thirst, continues in the gospels. In the synoptic gospels, the feeding of the multitude with a few loaves and fishes echoes Israel's story of being fed by God in the wilderness. In John's gospel, the connection becomes explicit. The Jesus of John refers to the story of manna in the wilderness and then speaks of himself as the true bread from heaven: "I am the bread of life; whoever comes to me will never be hungry."[34] Drink imagery is also used by John. In the story of the wedding at Cana, Jesus provides the wine that never runs out.[35] In Jesus' conversation with the Samaritan woman at the well, Jesus is one who gives "living water" and says, "Those who drink of the water that I will give them will never be thirsty."[36] Salvation is having one's thirst quenched, one's deepest hunger satisfied.

Salvation as Knowing God

Knowing God as an image of salvation does not mean knowing *about* God. Rather, it refers to direct, immediate knowing, as one knows a person in a relationship. Knowing God is implicit in some of the metaphors we have already considered, especially those related to seeing God and experiencing the love of God. It is explicit in a number of biblical texts. In Jeremiah, it is associated with the "new covenant" that God will make with Israel:

> No longer shall they teach one another, or say to each other, "Know the LORD," for *they shall all know me,* from the least of them to the greatest, says the LORD.[37]

Hosea's use of lover-beloved imagery to describe the divine–human relationship climaxes with "You shall *know* the LORD."[38] The gospel of John explicitly connects it to "eternal life": "This is eternal life: *to know God.*"[39] Noteworthy in John is the fact that "eternal life" is not simply or primarily in the future but is a present reality.[40] To know God is already an experience of "eternal life." The opposite of knowing God is, of course, not knowing God. In John, not knowing God is associated with images of being "in the dark." To know God is to be in the light. And thus knowing God and enlightenment are closely connected as images of salvation.

Salvation as the Kingdom of God

"Kingdom of God" is the most common image of salvation in the teaching of Jesus. We have already considered it in the previous chapter, but I include it again here because of its importance and because it underlines that biblical images of salvation include a communal and political dimension. For Jesus, the kingdom of God is both a social vision (and thus future) and a present reality (whose power is already at work and which can be known in the present).

As a social vision, it points to a way of living together in which, to use the language of the beatitudes, the destitute are blessed, and the hungry are filled.[41] As a present reality, the "kingdom of God" points to living under the kingship of God instead of under the kings and lords of this world. These rival lords are political, cultural, and psychological. The image thus connects to the exodus story as well: one is liberated from bondage to the lords of this world by living under the kingship of God.

As I conclude this section on biblical images of salvation, I want to emphasize that though I have treated them one by one, they are often combined in biblical texts and in our own experience. People under political and economic bondage often experience hunger and thirst as well; the rations for slaves in Egypt were meager. The exiles in Babylon were not only strangers in a strange land but also blind and deaf.[42] Bondage and sin can be combined: we are in bondage to anxious self-preoccupation and habituated and hurtful ways of being. We are anxious because of our exile and blindness, estranged from that to which we belong, and unable to see the presence of God around us. In short, treating these images separately should not lead to the inference that only or primarily one image will fit the experience of a particular individual. Rather, cumulatively they image the wounds of existence that need healing, the predicament from which we need deliverance.

Together, these images of salvation also make striking affirmations about God:

God wills our liberation, our exodus from Egypt.

God wills our reconciliation, our return from exile.

God wills our enlightenment, our seeing.

God wills our forgiveness, our release from sin and guilt.

God wills that we see ourselves as God's beloved.

God wills our resurrection, our passage from death to life.

God wills for us food and drink that satisfy our hunger and thirst.

God wills, comprehensively, our well-being—not just my well-being as an individual but the well-being of all of us and of the whole of creation.

In short, God wills our salvation, our healing, here on earth. The Christian life is about participating in the salvation of God.

THE GIFTS OF SALVATION

What the experience of salvation feels like is described with particular power by Paul. The gifts of the Spirit are "freedom, love, joy, peace, patience, kindness, generosity, faithfulness, gentleness, and self-control."[43] Four of these are most central in Paul's writings: freedom, joy, peace, and love. We are freed from anxious striving and from self-preoccupation. We experience the sheer joy of being, just as we experience the peace of being reconciled to ourselves, to each other, and to life itself. We experience the joy of being loved and the ability to love in the freedom and self-forgetfulness of faith.

One contemporary Pauline scholar uses a particularly arresting phrase to describe the Christian experience of salvation: it leads to the life of "erotic exuberance."[44] In order that this striking phrase not be misunderstood, I should emphasize that "erotic" here does not refer narrowly to sexual feeling, as it commonly does in the modern world, but means what *eros* meant in ancient Greek: the desire for union. Erotic exuberance refers to the joyful experience in which our estrangement is overcome and we are reunited with "what is"—with the world and with the one in whom we and the world live and move and have our being. Freedom, joy, peace, and love—a life marked by these is, it seems to me, enormously attractive. Who would not want this?

SALVATION BY GRACE THROUGH FAITH

How does salvation come about? And how do we participate in it? The answer suggested by the heading of this section discloses my Lutheran heritage: salvation comes by grace, and we participate in it through faith.

Grace

The genius of the Lutheran contribution to Christianity (in addition to its music and intellectual tradition) is its emphasis on grace. The emphasis flows out of the religious experience of Luther himself. After spending years of agony trying to be sufficiently righteous and pure to merit God's favor, Luther experienced radical grace: God's acceptance of him (and us) apart from our own works and effort. Yet though this claim shines forth with particular brilliance in the experience, preaching, and teaching of Luther, it is not idiosyncratic to him. He recovered an emphasis central in many Christian voices before him: in Augustine, in Paul, and more broadly in the biblical tradition.

Grace means that salvation comes from God. Grace means that salvation comes through divine initiative. So it is in the Bible: God led the Israelites out of Egypt, God empowered the return from exile, God is the source of light and sight, God takes the initiative in forgiveness, God loved (and loves) us long before we knew that (and whether we know that now or not), God gives new life to the dead, God is the source of being born again, God gives the bread of life and the living water.

The more one understands grace, the less self-righteous and self-made one can feel. Grace undermines all Christian pretensions to self-righteousness. It also undermines a common corollary of contemporary American individualism, the notion that I am what I am because of how hard I have worked. Even in secular terms, the notion that we are "self-made" is patently false. How much of our own "achievement" is because of our genetic inheritance, the family and economic circumstances into which we were born, and a myriad of events in our lives over which we have had very little control? And is it really true that those who have not done as well have only or mostly themselves to blame? Grace calls into question some of our most cherished religious and political beliefs. But properly understood, grace is a profoundly egalitarian notion. The more one understands grace, the more hubris (and its corollary of judgment of others) will be replaced by gratitude. Gratitude and grace go together.

Faith

Faith is the response to the divine initiative of grace. Faith is the human response to God. It is a rich notion, with several dimensions of meaning. To see these, we need to begin by clearing the ground of two common misunderstandings, both of which operated for several decades in my own Christian journey.

One of them, identified earlier in this book, sees faith within the framework of requirements. What God wants from us (in return for which we get salvation) is faith. Here faith becomes a "work," something we do that makes us right with God.

A second distortion of faith is a modern development. The Enlightenment of the seventeenth century called into question many common Christian beliefs, ranging from an earth-centered universe to supernatural miracles to a factually accurate Bible to the reality of God. Matters that had been taken for granted for centuries became questionable. In this situation, faith began to mean for many people "believing things that are pretty doubtful." Faith and knowledge become opposites; faith is what one turns to when knowledge runs out, and faith can even mean believing things that are contrary to knowledge. Moreover, the object of faith changed: from faith as faith *in God* to faith as faith in the truth of doctrinal claims and/or the Bible.

But this is not what faith meant historically in the biblical and Christian traditions. As the human response to God, it has three primary dimensions of meaning.[45]

First, there is *faith as fidelity,* or faithfulness. The home of the notion is a relationship: to have faith is to be faithful to the relationship with God. Faith as fidelity is the meaning of "the first commandment of all": "You shall love the Lord your God with all your heart, and with all your soul, and with all your mind, and with all your strength."[46] Faith as fidelity is the giving of one's heart, of one's self at its deepest level, to God.[47] Its opposite is not doubt but infidelity, or (as the prophets frequently spoke of it) adultery and idolatry.[48]

A second meaning is *faith as trust.* Once again, we see its meaning most clearly by thinking of a relationship. To have faith in somebody is to trust them; to have faith in God is to trust God. We see the meaning of faith as trust most clearly by considering its opposite: anxiety. In the famous passage about God's care for the birds of the air and the lilies of the field, Jesus linked lack of faith and anxiety: "Why are you anxious, O people of little faith?"[49] To the extent that we are anxious, we lack faith in God; growth in faith means becoming more trustful of the one in whom we live and move and have our being.

A third meaning is *faith as belief.* Faith does involve belief but only in a very general sense: namely, the belief that there's something to all of this. Faith as belief does not mean believing a particular set of doctrines or biblical statements to be true, regardless of their intelligibility or persuasiveness. But faith does involve believing enough to respond. The Hebrews in Egypt had to respond to the liberating act of God or they would have remained slaves; they had to believe enough to think that it was worthwhile to leave Egypt. But obviously what they believed was not a set of doctrinal claims or propositions; rather, they believed God.

The relationship among faith, knowledge, and belief is suggested by a story involving the famous depth psychologist Carl Jung. In the last year of his life, he was interviewed for a BBC television documentary. The interviewer asked him, "Dr. Jung, do you believe in God?" Jung said, "Believe? I do not believe in God—I know."[50] The point: the more one knows God, the less faith as belief is involved. But faith as belief still has a role: it can provide a basis for responding even when one does not know for sure, and it can also get one through periods of time in which firsthand experiences of God are lacking.

In addition to underlining that faith includes elements of fidelity, trust, and belief, there is one more comment to make. Namely, what is the relationship between faith and will? It is not a simple relationship. It seems clear to me that faith is not simply a matter of choice. It has not been so in my own experience. In my adolescence, when my doubt caused me great anguish, if I could have gotten rid of it by choosing to believe, I would gladly have done so. But I was not able to. Moreover, if we could get rid of our anxiety simply by choosing to be trustful, surely we would do so. Or if we could experience the gifts of salvation—freedom, joy, peace, and love—simply by choosing to have faith, who wouldn't do that?

Thus faith is not simply a matter of will. Instead, it seems to me, we are led into it. It grows. And the process continues throughout our lifetime. It is not a requirement that we are to meet but a quality that grows as our relationship with God deepens. Yet the will is also involved. We decide to take the first step, and then another (though sometimes we are virtually pushed into this by desperation or lured into it by example or experience). The will is involved in seeking to be faithful even when our faith is not immediately verified by our experience. So I do not think the will is absent in the life of faith.

Yet the connections between the work of the Spirit and our own response to the Spirit are so complex that one may legitimately speak of faith as both our response to God and as itself a gift of God. Once again the spiritual mentor of my childhood, Martin Luther, seems to me to speak wisdom. In his "Small Catechism," Luther said, "I believe that I cannot by my own reason or strength believe in Jesus Christ my Lord or come to him; but the Holy Spirit has called me through the gospel and enlightened me with His gifts." Even faith ultimately is a gift of God. It is by grace.

SALVATION AND AFTERLIFE

As I mentioned at the beginning of this chapter, when I was a child, I thought salvation was about going to heaven by believing in Jesus and Christianity. I no longer think that. But I do want to return to the question of an afterlife.[51] There is much that I do not know about it and do not have any beliefs about. In this sense I am an "agnostic" about an afterlife, in the specific technical sense of the word. "Agnostic" is from the Greek word for knowledge, *gnosis,* preceded by the negation *a-:* an agnostic is one who does not know.

Having said there is much about the afterlife that I do not know or have beliefs about, I nevertheless think there is something rather than nothing. I find the data collected about near-death experiences (NDEs) to be both intriguing and reasonably compelling. Too much should not be claimed; NDEs do not prove an afterlife. Whatever NDEs may disclose to us, they tell us only about what happens in the first seconds or minutes after clinical death. But they are suggestive. Though it is possible for a reductionist worldview to account for several typical features of NDEs, these experiences on the whole call into question the adequacy of such a worldview.

In particular, the out-of-body aspect of the experience, in which the person "sees" what is happening from a vantage point outside of his or her body (and what is seen is frequently confirmed later by other observers), suggests that consciousness can at least momentarily separate from the body. Again, this does not prove long-term survival after death, but it radically calls into question the materialistic worldview that is the major basis for modern skepticism about life after death.[52]

So I think that there is something beyond death rather than nothing. But I find it impossible to move beyond that very general affirmation to any detailed beliefs.

One reason is that I do not know how anybody can know about such matters. Nor can one resolve this state of not-knowing by believing: believing that something is true has nothing to do with whether or not it is true.

A second reason is the diversity of beliefs about the afterlife within the Christian tradition itself, which makes it impossible to speak of a standard Christian position about many afterlife questions. I provide some examples.

Does the afterlife begin at the moment of death or only at the end of time—that is, at the last judgment? Christians have believed both. For roughly the first thousand years, the dominant Christian belief was that the dead are simply dead until the last judgment. In the early Middle Ages, that belief began to be replaced by the belief that judgment occurs for each individual immediately after death.

Is entry into a blessed afterlife by grace, or is there a requirement? If there is a requirement, something we must do or believe, does this mean that Christianity (despite the language of grace) is really a religion of works? If it is by grace, then does everybody go to heaven? And if not, is that because God predestines some to heaven (and, implicitly or explicitly, others to hell)? One cannot resolve this dilemma by invoking the notion of "free will." If my participation in an afterlife is dependent on my free-will choice to respond to God, then my salvation is dependent on something I do. That makes a lot of common sense, of course, and most Christians have probably believed so; but this does mean that salvation is not simply by grace but involves a requirement. So: Is eternal life attained by grace or by works?

A related question: Is heaven only for Christians? That is, must one be a Christian in order to be saved for eternity? Much of Christian belief and practice through the centuries suggests so. For many Christians, it has been the primary motive for the missionary movement. Yet other Christians have balked at the notion. Can it be fair that the creator of the universe condemns large numbers of people to eternal punishment (or eternal nothingness) simply because they haven't heard of Christianity, or because the presentation of the Christian message in their neighborhood was unattractively done, or because they found their own religious tradition deeply satisfying?

Yet another related question: Are those who will participate in a blessed hereafter many or few? Scripture can be quoted in support of both notions, and Christians have believed both. Some Christians have believed in "universal salvation," on the grounds that nothing can ultimately resist the will of God or because of the logic of grace: if eternal salvation is a gift, then it must be given to everybody if one wishes to avoid the notion that God chooses some but not others. At the other extreme, some Christians have believed that only a few will be eternally saved. According to one twentieth-century sectarian movement, for example, only 144,000 will be saved, based on a literal reading of Revelation 7:4. Most Christians are probably somewhere between these two extremes and are content (properly, it seems to me) not to have a position.

Does the afterlife involve only heaven and hell or also the possibility of purgatory? Historically, Protestants have generally affirmed only the options of heaven and hell, but the great majority of Christians throughout Christian history have also believed in purgatory. Prior to the Reformation, it was a nearly universal Christian belief, and Catholic Christians still affirm it. Importantly, purgatory should not be associated primarily with punishment, as if it were short-term hell. Rather, as the meaning of "purgation" suggests, purgatory is an opportunity for further purification and transformation beyond death.

Behind this understanding is the notion that most of us cannot in one lifetime become sufficiently loving beings to live eternally in the presence of God. Rather than restrict heaven to the few, purgatory offers the possibility of progressive sanctification after death.[53] Functionally, purgatory and reincarnation are thus the same; both give us more than one chance to become fully compassionate beings. The primary difference is "where" this happens; reincarnation means further existence on the earthly plane of existence, while purgatory occurs on another plane of existence.[54] But to return to the matter of diversity of Christian beliefs about an afterlife: Is one, as a Christian, to believe in purgatory or not? The tradition yields no clear answer.

How much continuity is there between this life and the next? Will we have bodies of some kind? Will relationships persist? Will we "see" each other again? The language of popular Christianity throughout the centuries suggests so, especially at funerals and as a comfort to dying and bereaved persons. C. S. Lewis gently poked fun at this notion by speaking of it as heaven complete with cigars.[55]

But voices in the New Testament suggest considerable discontinuity rather than continuity. We see this in the exchange between Jesus and some Sadducees, an aristocratic group within Judaism who did not believe in an afterlife. Seeking to show that the notion of an afterlife made little sense, they told Jesus about a woman who was married to seven brothers in sequence, and then asked whose wife she would be in the life to come.[56] Their question makes sense if one presupposes considerable continuity between this life and the next. But Jesus' response points to considerable discontinuity: in the afterlife, "they neither marry nor are given in marriage, but are like the angels in heaven." What does that mean? Simply that there is no marriage or no sex? Or does it suggest more broadly that the afterlife is *very different?*

So also Paul: he speaks of the "physical body" as being quite different from the "spiritual body" with which the dead are raised.[57] How different are the two bodies? Is it simply that the former is mortal, the latter imperishable, but otherwise they are quite similar? Or to use Paul's analogy, is the difference as great as the difference between a seed and a full-grown plant?

To push the question of continuity and discontinuity one step further: Does awareness of personal identity persist into an afterlife? To make this personal and specific: Will Marcus know that he was or is Marcus, that he used to live in the Midwest and then in Oregon, and had a cat named Jenni? And if awareness of being this particular person does survive, would that be a superior or inferior state of affairs? Our natural impulse, I suspect, is to think that preservation of identity awareness would be a real plus; after all, isn't that what an afterlife is for, so that I, or we, can live forever?

But further reflection gives one pause. When I think of the best moments in my life thus far, they are moments when I was so wholly involved in the experience that there was no part of me left over being aware that it was me having the experience. That is, my best moments have been moments when awareness of being this particular person were not part of the experience. Given this, does it seem that preservation of identity awareness in an afterlife is important or even desirable?[58]

I mention these diverse beliefs and puzzlements about the afterlife not for the sake of undermining the notion but to suggest why it is that I am an agnostic about the details of an afterlife. I can't imagine knowing the answers to these questions, and choosing to believe one way or the other has nothing to do with how things might really be. We cannot solve not-knowing by believing.

Luther expressed our not-knowing about the details of an afterlife with a particularly apt analogy: we can know as much about life beyond death as a fetus traveling down the birth canal and about to be born can know about the world it is about to enter. How much is that? Nothing. Yet the analogy affirms that there is something at the end of the journey.

In the midst of this uncertainty, we can be confident of one thing: when we die, we do not die into nothingness but we die into God. The roots of the word *confidence* mean "what goes with faith" (*con* = with, *fides* = faith). Faith as trust in God includes the confidence that in Paul's words:

> If we live, we live to the Lord;
> and if we die, we die to the Lord.
> So then, whether we live or whether we die,
> we are the Lord's.[59]

It is the same confidence Paul expresses elsewhere:

> For I am sure that neither death, nor life, nor angels, nor principalities, nor things present, nor things to come, nor powers, nor height, nor depth, nor anything else in all creation, will be able to separate us from the love of God in Christ Jesus our Lord.[60]

But we can know what salvation means in this life. At the center of the biblical understanding of salvation is a relationship with God in the present, whose gifts are freedom, joy, peace, and love and whose fruits are compassion and justice.

This relationship with God, and all that flows from it, are the purpose of the Christian life. The invitation of the Christian gospel is to enter into that relationship in which our healing and wholeness lie, that relationship which transforms us by beginning to heal the wounds of existence and makes our lives in the here and now a life with God.

Notes

1. For the title of this chapter, I am indebted to Mary Sicilia, director of Christian education at Trinity Episcopal Cathedral in Portland, Oregon, who suggested it as the title of a lecture she invited me to give.

2. *The Compact Edition of the Oxford English Dictionary* (Oxford: Oxford University Press, 1971).

3. Specifically, Dan. 12.1–3.

4. Two clarifying remarks: prior to this time, the Bible speaks of exceptional individuals being taken to heaven at death (specifically, Enoch and Elijah), but this was not part of a general expectation of an afterlife for everybody. Second, the Hebrew Bible does speak of "Sheol," but "Sheol" does not point to an afterlife. Rather, "Sheol" is like the Greek "Hades": the land of the dead, to which everyone goes. It is not the equivalent of "hell," to which wicked individuals are sent to be punished. Rather, everybody goes to Sheol, a shadowy place and the home of shadows; as one of my professors put it in graduate school, Sheol (like Hades) is the place where the carbon copies of everybody who ever lived are kept. Thus, references to Sheol are not references to an afterlife in the usual sense of that word.

5. For life under "the powers," see especially Wink, *Engaging the Powers,* pp. 51–63, 87–104. Wink's exposition of the significance of "the powers" in the New Testament and their meaning for contemporary Christian life is masterful; in my judgment, this book is one of the most important works of New Testament theology in our time.

6. Luke 4.19. The importance of this idea is underscored by the fact that it is part of Jesus'"inaugural address," according to Luke.

7. Gal. 5.1.

8. An insight emphasized by Paul Tillich in his description of the human condition. See his *Systematic Theology,* vol. 2 (Chicago: University of Chicago Press, 1957), pp. 44–75.

9. See the magnificent language of Isaiah 40–55, spoken by an anonymous Hebrew prophet to the exiles in Babylon. Examples: 40.1–11, 26–31; 43.1–21; 44.1–8; 49.8–23; 52.1–10.

10. 2 Cor. 5.19.

11. See, for example, Eph. 2.11–22.

12. See Ps. 130.5.

13. Isa. 60.1–2.

14. Isa. 9.2.

15. Luke 1.78–79.

16. Ps. 119.105.

17. John 8.12.

18. Rev. 21.23, 22.5.

19. John 9.25. The phrase is perhaps most familiar to us from the hymn "Amazing Grace."

20. Job 42.5.

21. Mark 10.51.

22. John 8.12, 1.5.

23. John 1.5, 9.

24. For more on the superego and the monarchical model of God, see Chapter Three in this book.

25. For one of the most powerful statements of this notion, see Paul Tillich's sermon, "You Are Accepted," in *The Shaking of the Foundations* (New York: Charles Scribner's Sons, 1948), pp. 153–63.

26. Indeed, this is the core meaning of Jesus' death as a sacrifice for sins. To clarify, I (and many scholars) do not see "dying for the sins of the world" as Jesus' own purpose or intention or as something that God required; rather, it is a post-Easter interpretation of the death of Jesus using the metaphor of sacrifice. To say "Jesus died for our sins" and that he is "the once-and-for-all sacrifice for sin," as the letter to the Hebrews puts it, is to say that God has already taken care of our sins.

27. Isa. 43.4.

28. Bondi, *In Ordinary Time* (Nashville: Abingdon Press, 1996), pp. 22–23: "God loves us extravagantly, ridiculously, without limit or condition. God is in love with us; God is besotted with us. God yearns for us. God does not love us 'in spite of who we are' or 'for whom God knows we can become.'. . . God loves us, the very people we are."

29. Luke 9.60.

30. Eph. 2.1, 5; Col. 2.13.

31. Gal. 2.20.

32. John 11.25–26; 12.24; 14.6.

33. Isa. 55.1 and Prov. 9.1–6 (quoted words from verse 5).

34. John 6.25–59 (quoted words from verse 35).

35. John 2.1–11. This is the first scene in Jesus' public ministry, according to John. As such, it is John's way of saying, "The story of Jesus is a story about a wedding banquet at which the wine never runs out."

36. John 4.7–15.

37. Jer. 31.34.

38. Hos. 2.20.

39. John 17.3.

40. English translations sometimes obscure this. The Greek phrase translated "eternal life" (and in the King James Version as "everlasting life") does not mean life that begins after physical death and then lasts forever; rather it means "the life of the age to come." For John, *that* life is already known in the present, this side of physical death.

41. Luke 6.20–21. Compare to Matt. 5.3–12, in which some of these are "spiritualized": the destitute become "the poor in spirit," the hungry become those who "hunger and thirst for righteousness."

42. For example, Isa. 42.7, 18; 43.8.

43. Gal. 5.1, 13, 22–23.

44. Robin Scroggs, *Paul for a New Day* (Philadelphia: Fortress Press, 1977), pp. 24, 34.

45. For this section, see especially H. Richard Niebuhr's *Faith on Earth* (New Haven, CT: Yale University Press, 1989), published almost thirty years after his death and edited by his son Richard Reinhold Niebuhr. See also Paul Tillich, *Dynamics of Faith* (New York: Harper & Row, 1957).

46. Mark 12.28–30.

47. Faith as "giving one's heart to God" is the root meaning of the Latin word *credo,* from which we get the word *creed* and which is commonly translated as "I believe." Thus originally "I believe" did not mean faith as intellectual assent to a set of doctrinal claims but the commitment of a much deeper level of the self to God. See my *Meeting Jesus Again,* pp. 136–37, and Wilfred Cantwell Smith, *Faith and Belief* (Princeton, NJ: Princeton University Press, 1979), pp. 76–78.

48. Faith as fidelity includes obedience, but this does not mean meticulous obedience to a particular set of rules or commands, but listening and responding—the root of the word for obedience in Greek means "radical listening." Faith as fidelity to God includes listening to God.

49. Luke 12.22–31 = Matt. 6.25–33.

50. *Face to Face with Carl Jung.* I have not reviewed the video to make sure that I have quoted it exactly. But I am confident that it is an accurate paraphrase.

51. Among recent books about the afterlife, I recommend Hans Küng, *Eternal Life?,* trans. Edward Quinn (New York: Doubleday, 1984); Colleen McDannell and Bernhard Lang, *Heaven: A History* (New Haven, CT: Yale University Press, 1988); Tom Harpur, *Life after Death* (Toronto: McClelland and Stewart, 1991). See also the older work of John Baillie, *And the Life Everlasting* (New York: Charlers Scribner's Sons, 1933). For a nontheological treatment of recent research, see Arthur S. and Joyce Berger, *Fear of the Unknown* (Westport, CT: Praeger, 1995).

52. For readings about NDEs, see Chapter Two in this book, note 40. For a summary and evaluation, see Berger and Berger, *Fear of the Unknown,* pp. 63–72, 120–124.

53. See John Hick's use of this notion in his *Evil and the God of Love,* p. 383.

54. For reincarnation in the Christian tradition, see Geddes MacGregor, *Reincarnation in Christianity* (Wheaton, IL: Quest Books, 1978). Reincarnation was declared to be heretical by Pope Gregory VI around the year 600, but prior to that time, as MacGregor shows, several important Christian thinkers believed in reincarnation. My point is not to make a case for reincarnation but to suggest once again the diversity of Christian beliefs about an afterlife.

55. Lewis, *A Grief Observed* (New York: Bantam, 1976), pp. 28–29.

56. Mark 12.18–27.

57. 1 Cor. 15.35–57.

58. I owe this insight to Huston Smith, in Smith and David Ray Griffin, *Primordial Truth and Postmodern Theology* (Albany: State University of New York Press), pp. 66–67.

59. Rom. 14.8; used as one of the opening sentences in the burial service in the Episcopal *Book of Common Prayer*.

60. Rom. 8.38.